Investing for Recovery

FT Prentice Hall
FINANCIAL TIMES

In an increasingly competitive world, we believe it's quality of thinking that gives you the edge – an idea that opens new doors, a technique that solves a problem, or an insight that simply makes sense of it all. The more you know, the smarter and faster you can go.

That's why we work with the best minds in business and finance to bring cutting-edge thinking and best learning practice to a global market.

Under a range of leading imprints, including *Financial Times Prentice Hall*, we create world-class print publications and electronic products bringing our readers knowledge, skills and understanding which can be applied whether studying or at work.

To find out more about Pearson Education publications, or tell us about the books you'd like to find, you can visit us at **www.pearsoned.co.uk**

Investing
for Recovery

Making your capital grow in volatile markets

Charles Vintcent

Financial Times
Prentice Hall
is an imprint of

Harlow, England • London • New York • Boston • San Francisco • Toronto • Sydney • Singapore • Hong Kong
Tokyo • Seoul • Taipei • New Delhi • Cape Town • Madrid • Mexico City • Amsterdam • Munich • Paris • Milan

PEARSON EDUCATION LIMITED

Edinburgh Gate
Harlow CM20 2JE
Tel: +44 (0)1279 623623
Fax: +44 (0)1279 431059
Website: www.pearsoned.co.uk

First published in Great Britain in 2010

ISBN: 978-0-273-72998-3

British Library Cataloguing-in-Publication Data
A catalogue record for this book is available from the British Library

Library of Congress Cataloging-in-Publication Data
A catalog record for this book is available from the Library of Congress

10 9 8 7 6 5 4 3 2 1
14 13 12 11 10

Typeset in 9/13pt Stone Serif by 3
Printed and bound by Ashford Colour Press

The publisher's policy is to use paper manufactured from sustainable forests.

For Thomas

Contents

Publisher's acknowledgements

We are grateful to the following for permission to reproduce copyright material:

Figures 1.3, 4.1, 5.2–12, 8.1, 8.3, 8.5, 8.,6 8.7, 8.10, 8.11 from Updata plc, extracts from 'Banks threaten to withdraw support for Tiger Tiger' by Ben Harrington and 'BT to cut dividend on another 10,000 jobs' by Jonathan Russell, 12 April 2009 © Telegraph Media Group Limited, 2009; Table 3.1 from *Financial Times*; figures in Appendices from ADVFN – www.advfn.com is Europe's leading financial market website.

Every effort has been made by the publisher to obtain permission from the appropriate source to reproduce material which appears in this book. In some instances we may have been unable to trace the owners of copyright material and would appreciate any information that would enable us to do so.

Author's acknowledgements

I should like to thank particularly David Linton of Updata, and Clem Chambers of ADVFN for their help and provision of charts, data and analysis, without which this book would never have been written.

Introduction

Stock market prices go up – and they go down. Sometimes the rise or fall is limited to a few shares, occasionally the whole market is affected. The cyclical 'peak and trough' pattern (sometimes referred to as boom and bust) is as much a natural occurrence as night following day.

The strength and length of the rise or fall will vary considerably, as will the length of time it takes to recover from a deep depression, particularly when it affects most of the industrial world. The destructive effects on capital that occurred after the Wall Street crash of 1929 and the resulting depression lasted until the outbreak of war in 1939.

Human nature is fundamentally more optimistic than pessimistic, and whilst the desire for profit is as much part of the psychological make-up of the average person as is the desire to improve their quality of life, the motto that the private investor needs to remember is 'safety first'. This is even more important today because fundamental changes to the UK banking system are taking place as a result of the collapse of the stock markets throughout the world that started in 2008. Banks have had to be rescued because their directors had risked depositors' and shareholders' funds; chains of shops have closed down and gone into administration. Questions abound as to the relative strengths or weaknesses of the underlying credibility of loan stocks, both corporate and governmental.

Investors have seen their capital values sharply reduced, and people who relied on fixed income securities to pay the bills have seen their income fall substantially. It is not surprising that private investors are bemused and bewildered.

'What should I buy?' 'What is safe?' 'When is this recession going to end?' 'What should my investment strategy be in such unfamiliar circumstances?'

Asset allocation and risk analysis, both important tools, are even more relevant now since the crash of 2008, and will remain so as the market recovers. Furthermore, risk control becomes an ever more essential wealth preservative for the private investor. This book will show you how to use all three both strategically and tactically.

There are, and will be, plenty of opportunities to make money as the world adjusts to the changing ways of the markets, the altered roles of banks and financial institutions, and increased regulations. This book will show you how to find investment opportunities, how to carry out your own 'due diligence' to ensure that your selections have the necessary financial strength to survive temporary setbacks and, above all, how to preserve your hard-earned capital by limiting downside risk as far as possible.

Private portfolio building and management needs as much care and nursing as any new-born baby. So, if you want to protect your capital against the ravages of erosion by inflation, or risk of loss from poor stock selection, or bad underlying investment management in managed funds, this book will help you to achieve your objectives.

The stock market crash of 2008

This chapter will examine:

■ The causes and effects of the crash of 2008.

■ The changes and likely after-effects of the crash.

■ Increasing regulations and costs.

Changes in the stock market

The so-called credit crunch started to affect everyone in Britain in the autumn of 2008. At the same time the stock market crash began and it devastated wealth invested in stocks, shares, property and savings, across all levels of society. It is important to understand the whole picture to learn lessons for future investment strategies as well as how to evaluate and guard against such risks happening again, because they will. The destruction has had far-reaching effects on the whole of the banking system, as well as the size and burden of debt loaded on to the country that will change the approach to investment in the UK for many years to come. It did so after 1929 and it will happen again some time in the future.

The stock market crash of 2008, together with the breakdown in bank lending and the consequent crisis in liquidity produced knock-on effects that were deep and widespread. They forced the Treasury to guarantee the bad debts of Northern Rock and Bradford & Bingley, and the merger between Lloyds TSB Royal Bank of Scotland and Halifax Bank of Scotland. The threat to the retail banking system was real and very dangerous for the country.

Lending between banks almost ceased and the Bank of England was forced to reduce base rates to 0.5 per cent to try to get cash flowing again. In unprecedented moves, it cut rates six times in six months to a level that had never been seen since the Bank of England was founded in 1694. In addition to these measures, the Bank was driven to take action known in the market as 'quantitative easing'. This is a system whereby the Bank buys back Treasury bonds (government debt known as gilt-edged stock) and corporate loan stock to try to inject cash into the system to enable the stock holders to spend the cash by reinvesting, and thereby boosting the economy. The objective is to get cash flowing again. The best analogy is provision of a blood transfusion to someone who has haemorrhaged badly after a car crash, to enable the vital organs to continue to function. Quantitative easing is, in effect, printing money. Initially, it may well unlock the paralysis of credit that strangles industrial activity, but it causes inflation ultimately in so far as it is not backed by any increase in the underlying assets of the country. When the increase in money supply has achieved its objective, the onus will be on the Treasury and Bank of England to reduce the quantity of money in circulation to avoid the corrosive effect of inflation. Whether adequate action is taken when the time comes will depend on the political management of the economy then. I shall deal with the potential dangers this action can cause for the private investor when planning his or her investment strategies.

One of the results of the crash has been to turn the spotlight on the ways in which retail banks operated before the credit crisis. These examinations exposed interesting and important areas wherein enormous losses were sustained, and at the same time disclosed a substantial degree of ignorance by senior managements, which were considered by many to be negligent, in controlling the massive risks to the capital of individual banks as well as their customers' deposit funds.

The first tangible example of the dangers was the complete lack of control by senior management, and this was demonstrated by the spectacular collapse of Barings Bank in 1995 when a trader in the Far East lost the bank £827m speculating on futures contracts. Barings was a merchant bank (often called an investment bank nowadays), founded in 1762. It had built a reputation for competence and integrity over two hundred years. It was clear subsequently that the senior management in London neither understood the risks involved in these instruments, nor did it exert any control over its branch office on the other side of the world, although it enjoyed the seemingly large paper profits that appeared to be mounting fast.

The causes

An abundance of cheap money throughout the global banking system led to a massive growth in the provision of mortgage funds to house buyers, which in turn generated widespread fraudulent applications for mortgages. The ease of obtaining this low-cost finance led to a continuous rise in house prices and this upward spiral fed on itself so that property values became unrealistic in many areas of the UK and the US. The debt that this frenzied activity created became unsustainable and the result was the crash of 2008.

This led to a situation whereby neither the banks nor independent auditors could evaluate the extent of potential bad debts that were facing the financial industry. Asset values were meaningless. The old and often forgotten truism says that 'something (anything) is only worth whatever somebody is willing to pay for it at the time'. When the banks announced huge losses, people asked 'Where did all the money go?' Well, the banks paid large sums of money for 'bundles' of mortgages, all of which were supposed to produce a certain sum every month made up of part interest and part capital repayment. When, suddenly, Northern Rock was thought by the money markets to be overtrading, i.e. to have borrowed more money than its capital base allowed within the banking rules, it defaulted on its obligations. In the same way that a juggler keeps several balls in the air by repeatedly catching each one and throwing it back in the air in rotation, when one fell out of sequence it brought the rest down with it. This meant that the value of each 'bundle' fell like a stone and suddenly they were worth a lot less than the price at which they had been bought because no other bank wanted to buy them. The difference in value equates to the loss. If your house can only be sold for half the price you paid for it a year ago, you have 'lost' half of the value of your asset on paper. If you are forced to sell your house at that time, you do not have the luxury of being able to wait until the market turns back up again – you have to realise your loss and try to rebuild your capital, so your paper loss becomes an actual loss.

The effects

When the banks stopped lending, it affected corporate borrowers as well as private account holders. Mortgage funds dried up and small businesses found their overdraft facilities were not being renewed. People as well as business enterprises, other than government departments, stopped spending money. Corporate clients of the banks, and particularly the smaller businesses, started to lay off employees. Larger companies reduced the number of their staff as well, and in many cases they stopped sub-contracting work. Order books throughout the world collapsed.

The value of blue chip shares (equities, not gilts) fell in March 2009 to a level 47 per cent below their prices in October 2007. The price of gilts rose with a corresponding drop in yields, which hit savers hard.

The government has committed nearly £1 trillion of cash (one *million* million pounds, £1,000,000,000,000) in an attempt to kick-start the paralysed cash flow by underpinning the capital structures of the banks. The reason for the paralysis in cash flowing out from the banks into mortgages and commerce was because the initial volumes of assistance given to them by the government was being held back to cover their potential bad debts (called toxic debt). This huge liability had arisen as a result of the vicious spiral which started because of rising mortgage defaults; boosted by increasing unemployment; resulting from contracting order books caused by lack of spending in the retail and manufacturing and financial services industries; which was started by the reduction, and sometimes complete withdrawal of credit provided by the banks...

The massive debt incurred by the government was covered in the short term by printing money (quantitative easing), but in the long term it will have to be borne by the tax payer through increased imports because it will have to be repaid if Britain's international Triple A credit rating is to be maintained.

The UK government spent £94bn to prop up Royal Bank of Scotland, HBOS and Lloyds TSB as well as having nationalised Northern Rock and parts of Bradford & Bingley. Also, the Treasury and the Bank of England have pledged hundreds of billions of pounds of further support for the fragile banking system. A £250bn credit guarantee scheme announced in October 2009 was expanded to encourage banks to lend more. Figures 1.1 and 1.2 summarise the government's rescue plans.

Quite apart from the cost to the public, whether current or postponed, the list of casualties in the financial sector, both in the US and in Britain, could never have been imagined a year before the crash:

- Failed: Lehman Bros.
- Nationalised: Northern Rock, Bradford & Bingley.

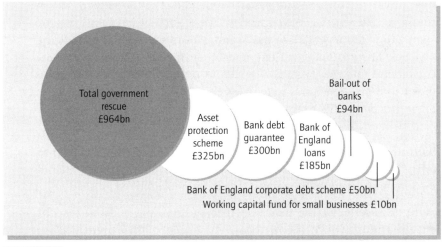

Source: Treasury, Bank of England, DBERR

figure 1.1 UK rescue plans

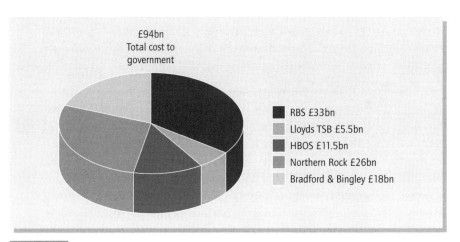

figure 1.2 Cost of bailing out the banks

■ Taken over: Merrill Lynch, Alliance & Leicester, HBOS, Bear Stearns.

■ Bailed out: LloydsTSB/RBS (Royal Bank of Scotland), Citi Bank, AIG, Bank of America, Freddie Mac, Fannie Mae.

The damage

The reduction in the base rate to 0.5 per cent by the Bank of England had three important effects. First, it lowered the cost of borrowing money substantially – if anyone was prepared to lend it. The corollary to that, of course, is that savers got even less by way of interest payments thereby eliminating any incentive to put spare cash into the banks or building societies. Many people who rely upon their savings to pay their living costs found that they were getting almost nothing by way of interest so they withdrew their funds to reinvest elsewhere to provide them with a higher income. This exacerbated the reduction in money available to lend for mortgages by the banks or building societies.

Second, it lowered the amount of interest that the government had to offer on future issues of gilt-edged stock (the coupon), and thus reduced the long-term yield that these instruments produce.

Third, as a result of the reduction in base rates, the demand for gilts increased and the prices followed suit, which reduced the current yields to maturity at the higher prices.

The size of the pension deficits facing some of Britain's biggest companies has jumped by around £100 billion to a record £390 billion. This may well drive companies to shut down their pension schemes – not only for future employees but for those already paying into them. *Making provision for additional pension income will become an essential part of financial planning for the private investor.*

It has long been one of the tenets of the investing public, and one that has been promoted by the managers of unit and investment trusts, that 'generally in the long term equities outperform government stocks and most other forms of investment'. This claim has been one of the main planks used by financial advisers when suggesting savings or investment schemes for retirement. Figure 1.3 is a graph of the FTSE 100 index over twenty-five years and shows how important timing is when deciding when to invest in equities, when to switch into gilts or other fixed interest securities, and the value of augmenting share purchases with some carefully controlled leveraged instruments used as 'insurance' against unexpected adverse price movements. I shall demonstrate in detail how to choose, monitor and control the risks involved in these strategies later in this book.

The FTSE 100 index on 1 March 1995 stood at 3,138. Anyone investing then would show a gain on 1 March 2009 of only 788 points, or 25 per cent over fourteen years! And that is without taking inflation into account. Anyone investing in 2000 or 2006 would be showing a massive capital loss.

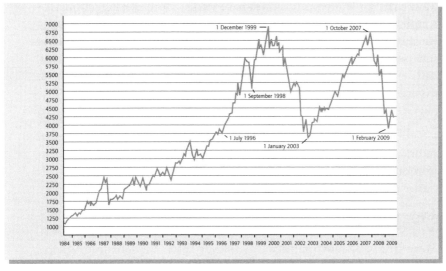

Figure 1.3   FTSE 100, 1984–2009   Source: Updata plc

This has been the worst ten-year period for equities since the 1970s, with total returns adjusted for inflation producing an average of 1.5 per cent a year. The effect will be disastrous for people under the age of 50 who are contributing into a pension fund or an endowment policy, with or without profit.

Over 600,000 people are expected to retire using one of these schemes in 2010.

The danger for anyone who is due to retire in the next five years at the very least is that the annuity rates will be very much lower than had ever been anticipated when the annual contributions were calculated, so that the actual annual amount paid by way of a pension will be considerably less than expected.

Clearly, the problem of making provision for any pension shortfall must feature highly when you are making plans for asset allocation and risk management in your portfolio strategy.

Damage to the mortgage supply chain

The unprecedented cut in base rates has produced winners and losers in the mortgage chain.

More than 3.5 million people who have tracker mortgages are paying substantially less each month and thousands of home owners are paying no interest at all. However, savers have been hit hard. Some banks have imposed a low limit on the amount that any saver is permitted to deposit each month. Returns on instant access savings have fallen from an average of 3.7 per cent to 0.36 per cent a year.

More than 8.5 million pensioners rely on interest from savings to top up a low weekly income. The building societies have reported a substantial outflow of deposits seeking a better return. The consequence of this reduction is that there is less money available to lend on new mortgages.

More regulations

There has been much criticism of the regulator, the Financial Services Authority (FSA), for not using its powers to force the banks to reduce their exposure to the risks inherent in trading such instruments in such huge quantities. The FSA has admitted to lapses in both the standards it applied and the lack of speed with which it reacted. The consequences will be much tighter and wider regulations that will be applied to all the financial service practitioners and this will include banks, insurance companies, stock brokers, insurance brokers, independent financial advisers and anyone giving any investment advice to the public.

Additional regulation will mean inevitably that the cost of administration and compliance, such as maintaining written records of all conversations and advice and risk warnings, will increase the charges to the private client, and will affect most those individuals with limited capital to invest.

Firms of stock brokers will be reluctant to offer a full advisory service to clients with capital available for investment of less than £200,000.

There are already plenty of varying charges for individual transactions made by private clients depending upon whether any advice is given; whether portfolios are valued; whether trading is done on an 'execution only' basis, and in some cases the level of some costs depends upon the number and value of trades bought and sold in a given period.

There is so much data available to the ordinary investor nowadays from stock exchanges throughout the world, including real time prices, which was only available to professional fund managers previously, so that you are perfectly well able to do your own research and manage your investments without needing too much advice from third parties.

It may be the case that the costs of regularly using financial institutions such as stock brokers or financial advisers becomes uneconomical. They probably will have to increase their costs for providing such services because they themselves are having to pay much higher charges for their services to fund the increased administrative demands imposed by the FSA, as well as the ballooning levies these institutions make to pay for their ever expanding number of employees. Consequently, the private investor will have to learn more about the art of investing as well as dealing directly with the market using execution-only intermediaries to make their stock market activities profitable.

Nevertheless, since it is true that costs are most unlikely to go down in the future, it is even more important for you, the private investor, to understand how to select and build a portfolio and control both the risks and the costs involved in investing directly in the stock market – that is what this book is all about.

When you are confident that you can interpret the signals that can be found on websites, and you know what and where to look for financial information as well as product and market data, you will probably opt for the services of an execution-only broker.

The next chapter explains what to look for that is likely to drive share prices up or down on the stock exchange so that you know where to look for the tell-tale signs of potential profit or loss and which allow you to increase your wealth, or control your risks and keep losses to a minimum. But before that, there is a potential danger of which you should be aware. It is called stagflation.

Stagflation

Everyone knows what inflation is, and the danger that it poses to your income and capital values. In Britain, people have lived with cyclical bouts of destructive inflation ever since the end of World War II. Inflation erodes the value of your income because it increases the costs of all goods. It leads to increased wage demands, which in turn drive up the costs of labour. All manufacturing and service providers are infected with the deadly growth of inflation and anyone who is reliant on a fixed income finds that life becomes steadily more and more expensive. It is a cancer that destroys wealth and can produce misery and hardship.

Stagflation is a term that was coined in the 1970s. It occurs when output remains stagnant, or declines, but inflation continues to rise, or is high already. It can be the precursor to deflation, which is even worse, and which is the long-term economic illness that Japan has been suffering for the past twelve years. The Japanese have had zero interest rates for many years now, and even that availability of cheap money has failed to get the financial stability that governments and businesses need so desperately.

There are many articles and schools of thought that blame the last bout of stagflation in Britain on the sudden and massive increase in the price of oil that occurred in 1974 and for which the Arab oil-producing countries have been blamed. Any substantial increase in the price of crude has an immediate and adverse knock-on effect on the price of nearly every item of manufactured product and service. It affects the costs of transport, energy production and heating, for example, and these also lead inevitably to higher wage demands as well. But whilst it is true that the price of crude oil was increased substantially in the 1970s, the facts behind this uplift are overlooked. In fact, the increase in the price of oil came at the end of a long chain of other price increases that have been largely ignored, but which were themselves the contributory factors that forced the oil price to readjust to its 'normal' position in the world economic structure.

Essentially, in the early 1970s, the oil price changed because of a three-year sustained increase in commodity prices which started in 1970. These commodities include the price of foodstuffs such as wheat and cereals, as well as raw materials such as copper, zinc and ores that are used in manu-facturing industries. Sustained increases in the price of oil are only possible under conditions where the market for the product maintains a steady and high demand. Sustained increased demand pushes up the price of the product in the market place.

It is likely that such conditions only exist when there is a rapidly growing volume of trade for all goods and services and there are long order books in the construction industry. Sales of consumer goods and services, such as cars, white goods, furniture, travel, clothes, and holiday homes, con-tinually surpass last year's record level.

These conditions are brought about by the widespread availability of cheap money. Governments control the supply of money and its cost through setting base interest rates, so when there is a glut of cash avail-able at very low costs, the main contributory factor is political rather than commercial.

If the money supply is increased at very low costs and if simultaneously there is low or declining output, the volume of government debt can get dangerously out of control and this creates a situation wherein taxpayers have to contribute to the reduction of this enormous debt mountain for many years to come. Taxpayers are corporate as well as individual, and the danger to commerce lies in the probability that any government that is intent on reducing the burden of debt will demand higher taxes when they see increased profits arising in company accounts, thereby inhibiting growth.

Summary

This chapter has identified the damage to which the money supply was subjected by the crash of 2008, in particular:

- The disappearance of several banking institutions.

- The consequent weakening of the banking system in Britain.

- The probability of increased regulation by the FSA, with corresponding increases in dealing costs for the private investor.

- The expected increase in the number of private investors wanting to do their own research using execution-only broking services.

- The erosion of the values of capital brought about by inflation.

2

Information: the lifeblood of all markets

This chapter discusses the factors that drive share prices in the stock market including:

■ The influence of information.

■ What constitutes insider dealing.

■ Economic pressures on the costs of money.

What drives share prices?

Before starting to explore strategies for investing for recovery, it really is important to remind ourselves of the principles that apply to the art of investing *successfully* in the stock market. These principles may be very well known to many of you, but they frequently get overlooked, or forgotten, and the old adage 'familiarity breeds contempt' should be borne to mind because it is very relevant in these changed circumstances.

You may well think that some of these points are elementary and wonder why I have included them in a book like this, and why I place such emphasis on their importance. It is because I have seen so many people lose money over and over again by ignoring these guidelines, as well as failing to remember the principles that should be second nature to an investor.

When I first came to work in the stock market thirty years ago, life was very much simpler than it is today. Unless you worked in a firm of stock brokers, or a merchant bank, there was no access to market data such as daily trading volumes of individual stocks or shares. There were no computers. There was no internet. Apart from the *Financial Times*, national daily newspapers devoted perhaps half a page to the stock market and only major company results would get a mention. The majority of the public were not particularly interested in the mechanics of the stock exchange, nor was there much 'educational' information generally available. The standard reply to the perennial question 'What makes a share price go up (or down)?' was 'More buyers than sellers (or vice versa)', and the motivation for being a buyer or a seller was either greed or fear.

But, as a generalisation and oversimplification, there is a deal of truth in those answers and they still apply today, in spite of the huge advances in technology and financial interest and thirst for knowledge, coupled with the availability of real-time data to the population at large. In fact, there is so much data being pumped out about trading and corporate reports and results, both actual and anticipated, that many private investors are bemused about what to use, or they are put off reading any of it.

Ask yourself 'Why do people buy a particular share?' The answer is because of earnings. The expectation that the earnings will increase attracts buyers. More buyers create an imbalance between supply and demand, which pushes up the price. When this situation occurs, commentators call it a virtuous circle. When it goes into reverse, and the supply exceeds demand it causes the share price to fall, which makes some of the holders of the share decide to cut any further loss to their capital invested and they swell the queue of sellers. These additional sales help to depress the share price even further, and so the process becomes a vicious circle.

Yet there are other reasons which can affect the price of any particular share, or sector, or even the market as a whole.

Uncertainty

It has always been true that the market abhors uncertainty, and it will always remain so. Private investors forget this at their peril. It applies just as much to markets in general, and sectors within a market, as it does to individual shares. It is one of the questions that any investor should ask him or herself: 'Is there any uncertainty about the company, its credit rating, its financial strength, its policies, its management, its products, its markets, its competition, or any other aspect that may have been criticised in the press or elsewhere within the last twelve months?'

There are many sources of data available to the private investor to enable him or her to check published material so there is no excuse for omitting such forensic detective work when you are carrying out your 'due diligence'. It is your money that will be put at risk, so you have only yourself to blame if you lose it because you did not bother to check the known facts.

Risk awareness

Very few private investors understand the need to become risk aware. In fact, this particular caveat or characteristic should become as automatic as the actions you take when you drive a car. It should be second nature and done subconsciously without you even being aware of 'doing the homework'.

This is not the same as risk control – I shall deal with that later. Risk awareness is making sure that you find out *why* a share price is moving up or down, or whether there is any reason why it *might* move up or down, so that you have a reason either to buy or sell or leave the share alone, or you are aware of a reason why it might move and you are prepared for it. A sudden substantial change in the volume of shares traded in a day will generally be the result of one or more of the following factors.

Greed

Greed comes into play from people not wanting to miss out on a rumour of a forthcoming rise in the price of a share. This often makes investors rush into a purchase without doing proper due diligence. Always remember the old adage: 'Where there's a tip, there's a tap.' Someone may be promoting a share because he bought at a lower price and if he can generate more than the normal demand, the price will go up. He gets out at a profit. If he sells a large number of shares at the higher price, the artificially ramped up demand will disappear and the price will fall back to its previous level, or below. If you bought at the higher price – you lose. Certainly, there can be occasions when you might hear some privileged information about a forthcoming event for a company. You might hear some loose talk from a person connected with the senior management of a company, for instance, such as an intended bid for another company, or the possible loss of a key manager or technician for unexpected reasons, or some news that is totally unexpected. Remember that it is illegal to buy or sell shares if you are privy to information that might be thought likely to have an adverse or beneficial effect on the price of the share if that knowledge was made public. This would be 'insider dealing', which is illegal. Any relevant statement or announcement made in the press or media before you buy or sell is considered to be in the public domain and therefore not 'inside information'.

You must always try to confirm or discount any rumour or 'tip' by cross-reference to other published information.

On the other hand, you might arrive at a conclusion about the future profitability of a company by doing your own detective work. You may discover some comment in a report published in a trade magazine or an obscure journal that has a very limited circulation and that could start you on a search to see whether any other source of data confirms your suspicions. Let me give you an example.

The pharmaceutical industry consists broadly of two main types of company.

- Drug manufacturers, such as AstraZeneca, GlaxoSmithKline (GSK), Eli Lilly, Merck and other world leaders. These companies are large and they sell their products internationally (sometimes by licensing local manufacturers in other countries). They also spend a great deal of money on research looking for products that they hope will be 'blockbusters', such as Zantac, which was the trade name given by GSK to its highly successful anti-ulcer drug often used in the treatment for indigestion and heartburn. This product earned GSK millions of pounds in the patent protection period of ten years after its invention. The drug manufacturers say that generally they expect one winner out of every ten new developments. The price of the new drug is kept high to contribute to the costs of research and development of other products.

- Generic drug manufacturers such as Shire, Bayer, and Procter & Gamble produce their own version of a successful product after the ten-year patent protection period has elapsed. They must include the main ingredient from the original formula, but since they do not have to fund any large research and development costs, they can sell the product much more cheaply and still generate good profits.

When a major brand drug manufacturer such as GSK has reported the initial launch and success of a product, such as Zantac, you should be aware of the fact that the protected life of the new drug will end in ten years. At that time you will expect the level of profits for GlaxoSmithKline to fall, unless they have been able to replace the reduction in their revenue stream by finding another blockbuster, and so you will expect the share price to fall. Since the drug has become accepted widely as an efficacious treatment for a very common complaint, it is a racing certainty that a generic drug manufacturer will adopt it and promote its own copycat product.

That would *not* be insider information.

If, however, you discovered the name of a generic drug manufacturer that was about to enter into a joint arrangement with GlaxoSmithKline to market a product that was very similar in its formula to Zantac, *and that information had not been reported anywhere in the press*, that *would* be insider information.

The lesson that this example gives is that when you decide to make a substantial investment in the shares of any company, you really do need to know as much as possible about the company, its products, its markets and its prospects before you lay your capital open to risks that could be considerable.

More buyers than sellers, or more sellers than buyers

When there are more people buying a share than there are selling it, the price will rise. Technology that is available to everyone in real time will show the volumes of each share that is traded on the London Stock Exchange during market hours as the day progresses. What it will not show are (a) whether the transactions are purchases or sales, and (b) the reasons behind each transaction. You will be able to work out the answer to (a) quite easily yourself. If the share price is falling, there are more sales than purchases; if the share price is rising, the purchases predominate.

There will be several possible reasons for the movement, and these are among the most common.

■ Expectation of good results. Everyone wants to see profits grow in the companies in which they have invested. Higher profits mean larger dividends and they produce an increased income. If there is an increase in the amount payable in dividend, the yield from the share will go up which will attract more buyers so the share price goes up in anticipation. However, you must remember the greed factor. Very often, press comment and analysts' forecasts overdo the expectations of profit and earnings per share, with the result that the market forces boost the share price too high. This is why the share price often falls when the results are actually announced, even though profits and earnings may be higher than they were previously. Greed has pushed the price up to an unrealistic level, and reality has been below expectations. Of course, if the results are the opposite to expectations, e.g. the company reports a loss when it was expected to report a profit, then the fall in the share price will be substantial.

Golden rule: the market always overreacts – up or down.

■ Admission to, or expulsion from, the FTSE 100. Periodically the London Stock Exchange reviews the companies that form the constituents of the FTSE 100. These companies are supposed to be the largest companies in the UK measured by market capitalisation (the number of ordinary shares in issue multiplied by the current share price). From time to time, some of the companies in the list decline in value whilst others outside the list increase and so a new list is issued. When this happens, the managers of the big tracker funds adjust their holdings within their portfolios and they will sell the shares of the companies that are being 'demoted', and buy shares in the companies that are promoted. These actions will be anticipated by the market and the relevant share prices will probably be adjusted accordingly.

Fear

Fear of acting can come from not wanting to take a loss on a share you have either just bought, or one you have held for some time. In the twenty-five years I spent as a private client stock broker I heard clients say 'I should have got out earlier' more times than I can remember. There is a natural reluctance to take a loss, which is quite understandable, but it is not the professional way to manage an investment portfolio. When all the signs indicate that the price has a strong probability of falling further, it is simply very sensible to stem the loss and accept it rather than go on hoping for a recovery. Haemorrhaging money is similar to losing blood if you have an accident and cut a vein. You don't wait for the wound to heal itself – you have to stop the bleeding.

If a share price changes direction downwards, and moves against the trend, sell it. The first cut is the cheapest cut.

Now let's consider the factors that make the markets either change direction, or accelerate the established trend.

Interest rate changes

The level of interest rate has a direct effect at all times on everyone; savers and borrowers, individuals, companies, local governments, institutions and so on. There is not a company anywhere, from sole trader to the largest corporation, that does not borrow money, one way or another, in small or large amounts, for periods ranging any time between overnight to several years.

If a central bank is going to make changes in base rates normally they are signalled well in advance. Usually any percentage increase or decrease is limited to relatively small amounts of, say, one-quarter or one-half per cent.

In the crash of 2008, the Bank of England reduced interest rates by 4.5 percentage points in six months to 0.5 per cent, which is a record low.

All increases in interest rates are inflationary and bad for share prices in the long term but they are good for annuity rates. All reductions in interest rates are good for share prices in the long term but they are bad for annuity rates.

Changes in bank base rates are a blunt instrument and they affect everyone equally and at the same time. The question of whether or not there is likely to be a change in the current base rate is so important that it must be addressed constantly by anyone managing financial investments as a part of continual risk assessment.

An essential part of any business budget includes a calculation of the cost of borrowed money in its profit forecasts every year. Such forecasts are constantly being modified in larger companies with alterations being made by comparing 'actual' against 'estimated'. Under normal circumstances there should be very little alteration needed to estimates as time passes because you would not expect interest rates to change that often. Nevertheless, an investor must always include the cost of short-term borrowing as an important factor when assessing a company with a view to adding their shares to the portfolio. Examples of how to recognise danger signals in the company accounts are given in Chapter 4.

The Bank of England has to assess what amount of interest payable should be attached to each issue of gilt-edged stock. This 'coupon', as it is called, has to remain unaltered for the life of the issue and is payable in tranches every six months until the stock is redeemed. If the coupon is set too high, it can become a millstone round the neck of the Treasury and the cost to the taxpayer is unnecessarily high. If it is set too low, the issue will not be attractive enough to the institutional buyers and the discount at which it has to be sold is overly large so that the Treasury does not receive sufficient proceeds from the sale of the gilt.

I shall explain in detail later on in the book just how this question of the relationship between interest rates and gilt prices affects long-term savings plans, such as pension funding, and how important it is when planning asset allocation by the private investor.

Government expenditure

Governments do not have any money. Whatever they spend running the country and giving away in aid to other countries or causes has to be obtained through tax. Income tax, corporation tax, capital gains tax, estate duty, road fund tax (which does not go towards the cost of construction nor to any maintenance of roads, for which it was originally raised), all fines, VAT, stamp duty, etc. The shortfall in revenue between monies raised by these impositions and the expenditure incurred by government has to be found by the sale of the debt to the public using an instrument known as Treasury Stock. These debts are effectively IOUs issued by the Bank of England on behalf of the Treasury and always they are offered in auction in denominations of £100 for a period predetermined at the issue date. On reaching that date (known as maturity) they will be redeemed by the Bank of England for cash at par value. They are known as gilt-edged securities. They are given this name because they are assumed to be 'safe as the Bank of England and the promise to repay them at par at maturity is gilt-edged'.

If government expenditure increases and at the same time the volume of revenue receipts declines, the amount of money needed to 'balance the books' increases and so the size of the gilt issue (government debt) increases. Although such debt that is raised today will not have to be repaid for several years, the debt will have to be funded and the only source the Treasury has for obtaining the money needed to repay the IOU at maturity is taxation.

Money invested into government debt is money taken out of current circulation. This reduces liquidity that might otherwise be available for other investments, such as supporting new issues.

In normal circumstances there is enough liquid cash that can be made available, either on call or at very short notice (e.g. 24–48 hours), or there are adequate credit facilities to cope with most unforeseen demands that might arise. Those who usually bid for government stock at auction are long-term investors such as pension funds, local council treasuries, managed income funds and trustees managing monies set aside for long-term financing requirements.

The threat of increased corporation tax makes corporate business management set aside larger amounts for provision against such demands from the Inland Revenue. This increased retention of cash can sometimes have unwelcome side effects. It can reduce the level of profits declared by the company, which generates the fear that its dividends may not be increased. They may even be reduced. If there is any possibility of either of these events happening, the share price will probably fall.

Changes proposed in legislation

Occasionally the government announces a major change in its proposed legislation that could have a substantial effect on society and consequently will be likely to alter or create a demand for goods or services. A good example is the current widespread preoccupation with energy saving and 'green' methods of energy production and transport systems and devices. If a contract is awarded to a particular manufacturer for the construction, say, of a nuclear power station, or an even bigger, quieter and more fuel efficient passenger aircraft, then the quick-witted investor will seek the names of the sub-contractors to those major constructors who are likely to benefit by receiving substantial orders which will provide work for their employees for several years.

New capital issues

When the shares of a company are first listed on a stock exchange, they are usually introduced by an offer for sale, or a 'placing' when a smaller quantity of the shares are made available to be traded on the open market. It is usual for the bigger companies to make an arrangement with a bank or large institution to underwrite the issue so that if, for any unforeseen reason, some of the new shares offered to the market are not taken up, the underwriters will absorb them at the offer price so that the market in these shares does not collapse shortly after they have made their debut.

Anyone who buys the new shares does so for one of two reasons. They may buy them as an investment for the longer term because they like the whole concept and believe that the company will prosper in the coming years. They think that they will get increasing earnings by way of larger dividends and this success will enhance the value of their capital over time. Or they buy them in the expectation of a very short-term gain. This short-term trading is known as 'stagging' a new issue. If there has been widespread good and bullish publicity before the issue, it will attract the stags because they will hope that the issue will be over subscribed and consequently there will be a good and sustained demand for the shares stemming from unsatisfied initial subscribers whose applications for shares were unsuccessful, and who will buy the shares in the aftermarket. (More buyers than sellers.) However, there are two risks attached to this practice of stagging.

First, you will not know how successful the offer was until after the lists have closed and the details are published as to how much stock (if any) was left with the underwriters. If there was a large quantity of shares not taken up by the market, the underwriters will want to sell them. They will not want to lose money over the whole operation so they will be unlikely to take any action that will depress the share price immediately, such as dumping large quantities of shares in the market. But they will dribble them out over an extended period by selling as many as possible without affecting the price adversely. This stock that is left with the underwriters is said to be 'overhanging' the market, and will act as a depressant for the share price for as long as it takes to clear the overhang.

Second, since it is impossible to find out what proportion of the successful applicants are stags, you do not know how far their profit taking (or loss cutting) will depress the share price. This situation can be exacerbated and last longer if there is a large chunk of shares overhanging the market from the underwriters as well. (More sellers than buyers.)

From the point of view of the investor, compared with the trader, this setback need not matter in the long run if the company is sound, well managed and has a good future. It can, however, be expensive for the trader, particularly if he or she has employed derivatives to make the trade and this is even more risky since there will be no trading history of the share price to indicate support levels.

Domino effect, or collateral damage

I explained earlier how share prices can fall if a company's results are worse than expected, but there is a side effect to this individual share price movement. A poor result in one share can cast a long shadow of doubt (and uncertainty) over the shares in other companies in the same sector. It may not be an actual poor performance that causes the initial rejection of the share, but something that might lead to a reduction in profits. For example, if the OPEC countries were to reduce the output of oil barrelage permitted to their members, it could be considered an inflationary factor in the price of crude oil since the supply would be restricted which would itself lead to an increase in the oil price. However, the reduction in supply might also lead to a reduction in sales of crude and therefore lower profits for the oil companies. This might cause investors to switch out of oil company shares, which will in turn lead to lower share prices.

Another example might be that a product from a pharmaceutical company was found to damage the health of an individual who had been prescribed the product, so there might be a strong possibility of very large financial damages being awarded to everyone who could be shown to have suffered from using the medication. The worry could easily become contagious and other pharmaceutical companies would come under scrutiny to see if there was any danger of their share price suffering a similar rejection. Such uncertainty will always damage share prices, even if it is only for a short time.

There is another factor that can often contribute to the velocity and depth of fall in one or more share prices in a sector. It has been brought about as a result of the markets becoming international and operating round the clock almost seven days each week. It stems from the widespread use of computers by the managers of the large investment companies that are responsible for making very large volume purchases and sales in most of the big international companies such as oils, banks, insurance, pharmaceuticals, aircraft, metals and other companies with very big market capitalisation values. To protect these managed funds from potentially catastrophic losses, their computers are programmed to issue sell orders automatically for predetermined large parcels of shares if the price falls below a certain level at any time. Sometimes, if the sell order is large enough, it will depress the price sufficiently to trigger yet another sell order. The further a share price falls, the more sell orders are issued by the computer until the entire holding has been liquidated. These are known in the market as programmed sales and they can have a deleterious effect on prices.

Since the crash of 2008 the stock market has become extremely volatile, and these triggers described above, or reasons for the movement in share prices, will have an abnormally large influence on the overall price levels every day. The picture that they will induce will be much more artificial than that which you would expect to see under a more settled and orderly market. Since they will continue to exert such a substantial effect for many months to come, it is even more important for the private investor that he or she understands the various roles that they play and that you satisfy yourselves as to the degree of risk that each one might play every time you are contemplating making a short-term trading investment. Re-evaluating the potential risk posed by each one should be an automatic part of your regular review of your long-term investment portfolio to see whether there has been a substantial change for the worse which might change your long-term strategy for one or more of your holdings.

Summary

In this chapter we have described the importance of:

- Having as much up-to-date knowledge as possible about the companies in which you are interested.
- The effects that greed, fear, and uncertainty can have on share prices.
- The way that government debt can strangle the market.

3

Risk evaluation

In this chapter we list some of the lessons to be learned from the fallout of the crash:

- Evaluating information from sources such as the press and company reports and accounts.

- Risk evaluation.

- The value of historical price data.

How will I know when the market has turned?

Whenever there is a significant and prolonged fall in the stock market, the behaviour patterns of investors remains generally the same. If the fall is dramatic and fast enough, people go through a predictable set of emotions and actions, and the crash of 2008 remained true to form.

In September 2008, the FTSE 100 was standing above 5,500 and by the middle of February 2009 it had fallen to 3,500.

After the initial reaction of amazement, followed by some paralysis and a reluctance to sell, many investors decided to go liquid and wait and see just how far the market would fall before going back into equities.

Because the Bank of England cut base rates to 0.5 per cent, many investors put some cash into government and corporate debt (gilts and company loan stock), which had the predictable effect of pushing up those prices and reducing their yields until they became unattractive investments. More a case of safety first rather than any anticipation of capital growth.

Needless to say, bank shares got thrashed and some such as Northern Rock, Bradford & Bingley and HBOS disappeared altogether.

In March, there was a minor rally largely because of the much publicised claims by the government that it was making billions of pounds available to the banks to overcome the refusal by the banks to resume lending and extend credit, and the announcement by the Bank of England that it would begin to employ quantitative easing to break the credit log jam.

The FTSE 100 rose to a level just above 4,120. Shares in Barclays had reached a low of 51p earlier in the year and investors thought there was an opportunity to grab a bargain. They were encouraged for two reasons. First, they thought the bank would survive and, second, that the bank would profit from its announcement that it would sell its iShares business. The share price rose because of the rally and investor interest. Several of the 'gurus' on both sides of the Atlantic, including Warren Buffett, were reported as saying that they thought the bear market had reached bottom and that even though the recovery might take some time, the only way for the market to go now was up!

By mid April, the FTSE 100 had fallen back to 3,983 and this time George Soros said the market was exhibiting all the symptoms of a bear market with the overall trend still being downwards. The reasons being that the economy had not been mended.

Now the 'gurus' were talking about the possibility of the FTSE 100 testing the 3,200 level. It last reached 3,287 in March 2003 and in 1995.

This is a classic example of a 'dead cat bounce' – so called because if you drop a dead cat from high enough, it will bounce just a little before falling back to earth once more.

You will know when the downward trend in the market has really stopped, and it will happen when everyone has finally given up hope of any recovery – ever! When the gloom becomes almost tangible; when the press and tipsters start to give the impression that there is no future in investing in equities, and when all hope seems finally to have disappeared. That is when it will turn. There will not be any fanfare or special event to tell you, but it will happen.

No one can say when the bottom has been reached. You will only know that when it has come and gone. You will be able to see it clearly on the charts after the nadir has become history, like water that has flowed under the bridge – take a look back at Figure 1.3 for some examples.

The market will remain very volatile for many months to come, and the result of the crash of 2008 together with the shortage of credit available to businesses throughout the world means that the dangers of incurring losses by the ordinary investor is even more apparent, and will remain so for a long time yet.

Lessons from the fallout of the crash of 2008

At the time of writing, there is no sight of when the world stock markets will turn. However, the spate of bad news about falling earnings, rising unemployment, reductions in the labour force, short-time working, company failures and rising debt is building up a head of steam among market commentators who are increasingly trying to reassure their clients and themselves that the green shoots of recovery are just around the corner. Some even hint that they might have discovered reasons in individual companies to get in now while the prices are so depressed. The inference being that there is much more likelihood of upside to the price than downside. I do not see any reason to follow such exhortations and I will show you the reasons why later in this chapter.

Meanwhile, here are some examples of lessons to be learned from the crash of 2008 that should be kept in mind when the euphoria and excitement of a recovering and rising market begins again.

When you do start to build your investment portfolio, it will be of paramount importance that you control your exposure to risk as far as possible, and understand how to equip yourself with as much relevant knowledge about your intended investments as you can.

Like any craftsman, to be effective you have to arm yourself with the best tools and understand what makes your trade tick. In this case, you need information and the ability to read the messages that are contained in both fundamental and technical analysis. It is not difficult, and with some regular practice you will be much better equipped to make a success of your stock picking as well as being confident in regular unemotional reviews of your investments like the professional fund managers do. Too many private investors become emotionally attached to their investments and find it difficult to cut them quickly when they stop achieving their targets. To select and control your portfolio efficiently you need sound information. You need enough reliable data without being swamped. You must feel that you are in control and that the time you spend in research is enjoyable.

Sources of news and data

I have found that the press coverage of business news in the *Telegraph*, the *Times* and the *Financial Times* is excellent, as it is in the *Investors Chronicle*. The online news business bulletins and reports are well covered by www.stockcube.com and they are a very useful source of informed comment. So too is www.advfn.com. I strongly recommend ADVFN as the best software program for carrying out the essential research into company results, financial ratios and key figures that you need, as well as giving you easy access to control analysis of your investments. It has the added advantage that the service is free. To maintain portfolio valuations and provide you with excellent technical analysis, including charting, you will find www.updata.co.uk the most user-friendly and extensive service. All are available via your PC, and it is no exaggeration to say that the information dispensed by these sources constitute 'the tools of your trade', without which you cannot hope to make serious money from the stock market. Clearly, whatever sources of reporting you choose to use, it is important that they give you accurate and reliable data. The sources that I have named always double-check the information upon which they base their articles or announcements and they are considered to be the best in the business. These tools will give you all the help and information you need to become a successful investor.

You will need to start by looking at the indicators that exist to guide your thinking and establish an approach to investment analysis that you will develop into your own system so that you do not overlook some of the essential checkpoints.

Indicators

Before we start to describe the indicators that you should look for when you start to build a portfolio for long-term investment, you need to start the discipline of automatically practising risk awareness, as well as risk evaluation.

Don't forget the old Sandhurst Royal Military Academy adage – 'Time spent on reconnaissance is seldom wasted.'

There are some developments in the progress of a company that contain the seeds of possible destruction in them, and you ought to be able to recognise those before they become fatal and beyond redemption. There are others which may seem to be crippling, but which on better and deeper evaluation are more like a short-lived attack of influenza and which can often offer a very useful opportunity for a quick profit.

Some of these indicators will be found in the press, some from company reports and accounts, some from online news bulletins and analysts.

Let me give you some examples, and demonstrate the thought processes that you need to train yourself to follow so that you get the full benefit from the published data.

The press

These two examples are by no means exhaustive, but I have chosen them to illustrate two typical announcements that should start bells ringing immediately you see them. You may not be an investor in any of the companies you read about but the announcement concerning BT should be noted in case you might contemplate making an investment in the share at some date in the future. Any adverse news such as is illustrated in these two cases should trigger some research into any other companies involved in similar business in which you have an interest or could be contemplating making an investment.

example 3.1

The following headline appeared in the *Sunday Telegraph* on 12 April 2009:

Banks threaten to withdraw support for Tiger Tiger

The owners of Tiger Tiger, one of Britain's largest bar chains, are heading for crunch talks with landlords in an attempt to avert the collapse of the business and save thousands of jobs.

The report goes on to state that the management of the company wrote to its landlords the previous week asking for rent cuts as a last-ditch request. In the letter, the management said 'the company's senior lenders (Royal Bank of Scotland and Barclays) were making any ongoing support conditional upon the achievement of cost efficiencies'.

This announcement contains a great deal of information and it should give a potential investor considerable cause for thought as well as making him or her very wary.

Even though the holding company that controls Tiger Tiger is a private company whose shares are not listed on any UK stock exchange or market, the announcement serves a useful purpose here to demonstrate the sort of message that should alert you.

These are the main points to consider when you see a statement like this.

First, it is now standard practice for all companies' banks to review the terms and conditions on which they are prepared to renew loan or overdraft facilities every year. A direct result of the effects the crash of 2008 has had upon the banks is that in nearly every case on the next anniversary of the review they lay down conditions under which they will provide financial support, and they often make the company enter into covenants as a condition for providing any overdraft or loan facilities (loans are usually accompanied by a charge, secured on specific assets, or unsecured and 'floating' over all the assets). If the company exceeds these limits even by a very small amount it will be deemed to be in breach of its covenants and the bank(s) can demand instant repayment of all outstanding loan or overdraft. If that happens, the company will probably not be able to pay any wages or creditors, and will have to cease trading immediately. Any such action that could take a great deal of control away from the board of directors does not bode well for shareholders. It signifies a substantial change in the circumstances that pertained when investors bought shares in the company. The practice by the banks of insisting on creating covenants as a condition of providing loan facilities is not new, but it has become much more frequently demanded. The problem for the private investor is that it is extremely difficult to find out whether any such covenants exist, or when they are suddenly imposed. Current accepted practice adopts the view that any such imposition of restrictions by the bank does not need to be reported to the shareholders if such actions can be considered to be standard operating practice by the banks in the normal course of business. Nevertheless, I believe that this poses a potential considerable risk for shareholders because the way in which each bank branch exercises its ability to act in a draconian way can vary enormously and there does not seem to be any published code of conduct. The imposition of covenants adds to the list of uncertainties.

Second, cost efficiencies are another tool in the armoury of the banks which they impose on company managements. These include the requirement that there must be adequate interest cover being generated in the net revenue stream shown in the management accounts. A general level of interest cover imposed is a minimum of three times the cost of the interest payable on the loans and overdraft. Such a demand could present a problem with cash flow for a manufacturing company with a long process lead time between having to pay for the purchase of raw materials and the conversion to finished goods and receipt of payment. You can see why it is important to understand as much as possible about the potential risks to your capital in every investment that you make and the need to satisfy yourself that the management is completely in control of the financial health of each company.

example 3.2

The following headline also appeared in the *Sunday Telegraph* on 12 April 2009:

Telecoms giant BT is preparing to cut another 10,000 jobs and slash its dividend when it announces preliminary results next month

This announcement, which included the intention to write down asset values by £1.5bn, will probably produce an immediate downward pressure on the share price for the following reasons:

- A writedown of asset values will have to deplete the company's reserves, which reduces the net asset value (NAV) per share. It is, in effect, a reduction in capital. Such an action is a negative move and you would expect it to have an adverse effect on the share price. In this case, the amount of money involved is very large and so the first thing an actual or potential investor should do is to examine the last set of accounts.

- A cut in the dividend is also a negative move, and you can expect a lot of shares will be sold as a consequence. The reason is because there will be substantial holdings of this share in the portfolios of pension funds, and if the yield is going to be reduced, they will want to replace their investment with another share that restores the income stream that will diminish as a result of the dividend reduction. It is well worth remembering two facts about pension funds. They tend to place the bulk of their investments in the shares in companies that form the constituents of the FTSE 100, because these companies have generally been considered in the past to be the safest investments. Also, pension funds are much more concerned with maintaining the highest income by way of dividends commensurate with safety. A pension fund has precise commitments to pay out on known dates in the future, and it cannot rely on capital growth to meet these obligations. Expectations of capital growth in equity investments never feature in the calculations of cash flow requirements by a pension fund. If the income from any investment looks as if it is going to be reduced, the fund will switch out of that share.

A reduction in the workforce, however, will be regarded as a positive move. It is a fact that in well over 90 per cent of companies, the most expensive item in the profit and loss account is wages. Added to wages and salaries are such additional expenses as National Insurance contributions, pension fund contributions, administration costs and general expenses associated with employees. A substantial reduction in the workforce will have an immediate beneficial affect on the overall cost of operating the business. You would expect to see the share price react positively to such news.

The market is unforgiving of any company that cuts its dividend, particularly a large one that is a member of the elite FTSE 100. It will probably remember this dividend cut for at least seven years.

In this case, because the company is very large, it may be possible to make a quick profit from such an announcement. More often than not, the market overreacts and the share price is marked down savagely in anticipation of an avalanche of sell orders resulting from the unexpectedly bad news.

Depending on the 'track' of the share price recently it may well be worth a short-term trade perhaps using a CFD (contract for difference and taking advantage of the considerable gearing that these instruments offer), because if the market has overreacted, it will reverse direction and recover several points in a very short time.

Company reports and the chairman's statement

There is a constant flow in the press of news items, as opposed to opinions, and company reports and accounts. Most of the larger companies publish quarterly or half-yearly figures. It may be that these figures are unaudited, but they will be near enough to give you a very clear indication of the way a company is progressing. The year-end figures will certainly be audited, and the report will contain a statement made by the chairman and probably the chief executive (or managing director) also.

You ought to see positive and bullish statements about the expectations of the company's performance in these reports. Any comments such as 'it is hoped that the expenditure of £XYZ,000 on a new computer will show a positive contribution to profits over the next few years...' should make you think of selling the share immediately. Check to see if there has been any adverse comment in the press concerning the announcement of this item and the way in which it was reported. You can always get copies of any company's report and accounts by writing to the company secretary.

You do not have to be registered as a shareholder, nor do you have to have bought any shares to qualify for this service.

Remember that published accounts take time to prepare, particularly the year-end figures since they must be audited. Normally it takes three months from the date of the company's year end before they are released, by which time they are somewhat dated. Remember also that any set of accounts is rather like a still photograph of a horse in the middle of a race. They show a 'picture' of the company's activities frozen at a particular moment. They do not show any of the company's progress since that date.

We shall deal in detail with the ratios that you can extract easily from the accounts of a company in the next chapter, under the heading of Fundamental analysis. These ratios are very good indicators as to the financial health of a company and the efficacy of its management, when you are choosing investments for holding long term, as well as for monitoring them in your regular reviews.

In really volatile markets such as have existed since the crash of 2008 you need a more sensitive and up-to-date flow of data for your risk control purposes. This is where technical analysis plays such a vital role in your daily tool kit for investing and risk control.

Share price movement

The best and most immediate indicator is the movement of a share price. As I have said earlier the share price moves directly as a result of the laws of supply and demand. More demand, the price goes up. Over-supply and the price goes down. When you see a rising price, you need do nothing. When you see a falling price it should make you pause for thought.

■ If the price falls a few pence (or a small percentage), it should go on to your 'watch list' for checking about twice a day. The first question you should ask is whether there has been an announcement from the company, such as quarterly, half-yearly or annual results. A fall in the price will probably be the result of disappointed 'greedy' short-term buyers getting out because they were expecting even higher earnings. If there is a bigger fall, and it subsequently proves to be for the same reason, that is a clear indication that the company's shares are overpriced (sustained excessive demand) and you should certainly sell. Technical analysis will give you a clear indication as to whether this is probably the reason.

■ You should check the yield that the share is producing compared with the average percentage yield for the sector (Figure 3.1). If it is much lower than average, this means that the share price is high in relation to its dividend (thus a low yield) and it is probable that the share price has been chased up by speculative buyers who think that earnings are very likely to increase substantially in the short term. Either they have got bored with waiting, or the fall is a result of widespread profit-taking by those who bought at a much lower figure.

■ You should check the price earnings ratio (PE) and compare it with the average for the sector (Figure 3.1). If the PE ratio is higher than average, it will confirm the deductions associated with a low yield figure (described above). If the PE ratio is higher than average, the reason is probably because the market considers the company to be more risky than others in the sector. Short-term speculation and quick profit-taking is thus more likely to be the cause.

■ Problems related to corporate debt could be another reason, as we have discussed above.

While the stock market remains so volatile, the risk of loss is much greater.

Market indices and daily trading volumes

Whenever you look at a chart of a market index, or a share price, or a currency or commodity, there is one overriding golden rule: *Always look first at the record as far back in the past as possible.*

This is because it will:

■ immediately show you the overall trend of the instrument and its direction.

■ enable you to measure the velocity of the rises and/or falls.

■ let you establish highs and lows.

■ show you the resistance levels and support levels.

■ show you the significant patterns and the frequencies with which they have occurred.

■ put the overall picture into perspective against which you can measure current short-term movement.

If you do not look initially at the long-term picture, you will be at a huge disadvantage.

FTSE ACTUARIES SHARE INDICES

UK SERIES

Produced in conjunction with the Faculty and Institute of Actuaries

www.ft.com/equities

	£ Stlg Mar 20	Day's chge%	Euro Index	£ Stlg Mar 19	£ Stlg Mar 18	Year ago	Div. yield%	Cover	P/E ratio	Xd adj	Total Return
FTSE 100 (100)	3842.8	+0.7	3192.4	3816.9	3805.0	5495.2	5.37	2.29	8.13	49.11	2358.50
FTSE 250 (250)	6272.4	+0.2	5210.7	6261.6	6191.7	9448.4	4.18	1.99	12.00	32.41	3624.51
FTSE 250 ex Inv Co (200)	6499.4	+0.1	5399.2	6490.0	6388.4	9768.6	4.48	2.07	10.79	30.67	3810.17
FTSE 350 (350)	1992.8	+0.6	1655.5	1980.4	1972.5	2871.7	5.24	2.26	8.43	23.78	2485.59
FTSE 350 ex Inv Co (299)	1985.0	+0.6	1649.0	1972.6	1963.9	2859.2	5.29	2.27	8.32	23.89	1272.74
FTSE 350 Higher Yield (130)	2179.1	-0.1	1810.3	2182.4	2183.6	3191.2	6.72	1.92	7.75	30.27	2565.25
FTSE 350 Lower Yield (220)	1683.8	+1.5	1398.8	1658.3	1642.7	2403.1	3.51	3.03	9.41	16.29	1535.27
FTSE SmallCap (258)	1705.6	+0.2	1416.90	1702.32	1689.09	2978.29	5.44	0.55	33.23	9.14	1948.70
FTSE SmallCap ex Inv Co (165)	1403.9	+0.5	1166.25	1397.19	138	2658.16	6.90	0.31	46.28	7.51	1659.47
FTSE All-Share (608)	1942.9	+0.6	1614.03	1931.04	1923.11	2814.01	5.24	2.23	8.56	22.93	2454.91
FTSE All-Share ex Inv Co (464)	1932.8	+0.6	1605.63	1920.73	1912.11	2796.52	5.31	2.24	8.40	23.10	1260.56
FTSE All-Share ex Multinationals (551)	554.7	+0.7	381.89	550.95	548.06	941.70	5.20	1.51	12.75	2.83	757.24
FTSE Fledgling (206)	2398.2	+1.2	1992.24	2368.73	2352.76	3585.76	6.94	0.30	47.71	16.95	3616.11
FTSE Fledgling ex Inv Co (135)	2669.0	+1.9	2217.21	2618.80	2595.39	4105.54	8.74	0.04	80.00†	13.26	3925.14
FTSE All-Small (464)	1166.4	+0.3	968.96	1162.49	1153.61	1995.84	5.65	0.51	34.68	6.53	1711.46
FTSE All-Small ex Inv Co (300)	1021.8	+0.7	848.87	1015.01	1002.99	1885.34	7.15	0.27	52.12	5.41	1532.86
FTSE AIM All-Share (1032)	396.0	+1.0	329.0	392.0	385.3	939.5	2.03	2.04	24.20	0.78	397.66

FTSE Sector Indices											
Oil & Gas (23)	7002.0	+0.8	5816.76	6944.59	6919.35	7340.17	4.81	3.01	6.90	100.75	4483.28
Oil & Gas Producers (17)	6735.6	+0.9	5595.44	6674.82	6655.91	7000.79	4.87	3.01	6.83	99.04	4446.26
Oil Equipment Services (6)	10131.1	-2.8	8416.20	10427.86	10023.02	15137.21	1.98	3.42	14.73		6182.14
Basic Materials (28)	3564.0	+3.1	2960.76	3455.52	3175.89	6587.05	3.46	7.32	3.95	42.98	2923.56
Chemicals (5)	3156.1	-0.3	2621.83	3164.57	3053.44	5040.45	3.85	2.65	9.82	9.49	2300.65
Forestry & Paper (1)	1907.0	+4.0	1584.21	1833.55	1854.12	4757.24	6.95	2.58	5.58		1595.89
Industrial Metals (4)	2749.2	+1.8	2283.88	2701.45	2468.38	8326.94	1.35	3.27	22.74		2192.37
Mining (18)	11295.0	+3.3	9383.12	10935.75	10024.39	20732.93	3.44	7.60	3.83	142.57	4823.53
Industrials (122)	1764.6	-1.6	1465.87	1736.84	1754.47	2519.25	4.26	1.74	13.51	4.08	1459.38
Construction & Materials (11)	3180.7	-0.2	2642.27	3187.14	3188.93	5114.14	4.79	2.46	8.49	8.95	2494.09
Aerospace & Defense (11)	2469.8	+2.5	2051.75	2409.17	2489.79	3348.81	4.12	0.74	32.82	5.08	2157.30
General Industrials (7)	1235.4	+1.9	1026.28	1212.94	1217.37	1868.43	6.27	1.64	9.72	2.34	1072.08
Electronic & Electrical Equipment (11)	1129.5	-1.6	938.33	1147.46	1136.04	2072.49	6.24	2.16	7.42	5.78	836.28
Industrial Engineering (14)	2324.8	+0.1	1931.27	2322.28	2272.01	3312.30	5.98	2.08	8.04		2231.72
Industrial Transportation (9)	1883.8	+3.2	1564.92	1825.86	1796.41	3569.77	6.33	0.72	21.83	27.47	1215.79
Support Services (59)	2548.9	+1.4	2117.48	2512.73	2520.82	3570.99	3.43	2.48	11.75	5.39	2160.16
Consumer Goods (36)	6491.1	+0.4	5392.32	6463.86	6670.37	8442.27	4.45	1.44	15.64	117.51	3675.75
Automobiles & Parts (1)	1112.2	-3.5	923.98	1152.69	1104.15	4469.19	6.51	0.55	27.73		886.13
Beverages (5)	5093.0	+0.4	4230.92	5070.67	5235.25	6368.48	4.47	1.90	11.80	58.83	2893.68
Food Producers (13)	3148.3	-0.6	2615.43	3167.04	3276.53	4390.38	4.54	2.68	8.20	1.92	2099.37
Household Goods (11)	4162.4	-1.0	3457.84	4205.60	4309.38	5370.24	3.40	‡	‡	63.78	2382.55
Leisure Goods (2)	1124.2	+12.1	933.93	1003.24	962.44	1869.32	4.41	‡	‡		749.71
Personal Goods (3)	4707.0	-0.5	3910.21	4731.98	4765.66	6194.84	3.23	2.50	12.38	14.85	2630.82
Tobacco (2)	19636.8	+1.8	16312.94	19293.14	19982.08	24341.73	4.91	1.13	17.94	682.80	9058.03
Health Care (22)	4887.1	+1.0	4059.87	4839.69	5029.72	4959.25	4.91	1.89	10.79	122.32	2678.12
Health Care Equipment & Services (7)	2546.4	-1.8	2115.38	2592.84	2662.32	4202.76	2.00	3.37	14.82	2.09	1908.34
Pharmaceuticals & Biotechnology (15)	5802.7	+1.1	5651.21	6727.01	6995.55	6693.30	5.06	1.86	10.64	178.68	3278.32
Consumer Service (91)	2302.5	-0.2	1912.74	2306.75	2305.52	3051.77	4.41	2.39	9.50	8.09	1685.24
Food & Drug Retailers (5)	3930.5	-0.9	3265.23	3964.57	4080.62	4632.59	3.40	2.21	13.31		3511.36
General Retailers (26)	1155.6	-0.8	959.96	1165.18	1121.03	1561.14	6.22	1.92	8.39	1.69	1026.48
Media (25)	2604.6	+0.3	2163.69	2595.80	2597.09	3504.00	4.21	2.11	11.24	4.21	1238.35
Travel & Leisure (35)	2899.6	+0.6	2408.81	2882.23	2829.23	4299.24	4.82	3.25	6.39	34.63	2223.95
Telecommunications (7)	1806.1	-0.7	1500.35	1819.18	1853.22	2403.81	7.25	1.61	8.57		1328.91
Fixed Line Telecommunications (5)	1387.4	-0.7	1152.55	1396.77	1365.53	2687.27	13.61	1.07	6.87		918.56
Mobile Telecommunications (2)	2743.6	-0.7	2279.20	2763.77	2833.75	3384.35	6.23	1.80	8.92		1750.45
Utilities (9)	5300.6	+3.5	4403.34	5120.23	5308.35	6487.80	5.89	0.98	17.25	21.04	3939.62
Electricity (3)	6230.4	+5.9	5175.81	5884.29	5998.76	7283.16	5.72	1.66	10.56	70.48	5696.60
Gas Water & Multiutilities (6)	4740.3	+2.5	3937.90	4624.56	4829.01	5894.23	5.96	0.70	24.06	3.28	3559.34
Financials (242)	2251.0	-0.9	1869.94	2271.68	2177.89	5285.28	7.47	1.39	9.61	29.51	1567.89
Banks (5)	2525.5	-4.5	2097.99	2644.42	2496.54	7516.80	8.51	1.90	6.18	41.83	1406.30
Nonlife Insurance (11)	1363.1	-0.6	1132.38	1370.84	1397.46	1312.71	5.74	1.94	9.00	28.05	1720.12
Life Insurance/Assurance (9)	2289.2	+10.9	1901.67	2064.89	1912.11	4754.36	8.65	‡	‡	15.79	1547.00
Real Estate (42)	1355.3	-	1125.91	1355.95	1281.39	3504.71	8.57	‡	‡	27.42	1218.60
General Financial (31)	2919.5	+2.1	2425.33	2860.11	2750.73	5461.85	8.03	1.96	6.37	20.72	2407.43
Equity Investment Instruments (144)	3632.0	+0.1	3017.23	3627.64	3661.04	5450.83	2.83	1.37	25.84	23.34	1629.69
Non Financials (366)	2321.9	+1.0	1928.89	2299.85	2308.51	2943.17	4.75	2.52	8.36	26.73	2564.56
Technology (28)	325.5	-0.2	270.39	326.13	324.33	352.67	2.07	3.57	13.56	2.29	370.11
Software & Computer Services (19)	427.8	-0.1	355.39	428.12	423.32	465.43	2.14	3.43	13.65	3.54	494.35
Technology Hardware & Equipment (9)	246.9	-0.8	205.07	248.73	253.70	260.18	1.75	4.33	13.16	0.40	265.51

Hourly movements	8.03	9.00	10.00	11.00	12.00	13.00	14.00	15.00	16.00	High/day	Low/day
FTSE 100	3786.4	3817.9	3800.7	3798.0	3820.6	3830.9	3827.7	3853.2	3820.8	3854.9	3778.9
FTSE 250	6245.2	6265.6	6221.0	6234.9	6232.7	6251.1	6235.6	6260.0	6239.3	6273.8	6200.3
FTSE SmallCap	1701.18	1699.28	1697.26	1695.50	1695.95	1698.55	1701.57	1706.85	1711.50	1714.42	1695.07
FTSE All-Share	1917.00	1931.53	1922.39	1921.64	1931.55	1936.75	1934.91	1947.06	1932.20	1947.06	1912.11

Time of FTSE 100 Day's high: 13:31:15 Day's low: 10:18:00 FTSE 100 2005/06 High: 6479.4 (03/01/2008) Low: 3512.1 (03/03/2009)
Time of FTSE All-ShareDay's high: 15:00:00 Day's low: 10:18:00 FTSE 100 2005/06 High: 3291.47 (03/01/2008) Low: 1781.64 (03/03/2009)

Further information is available on http://www.ftse.com © FTSE International Limited. 2008. All Rights reserved. "FTSE", "FT-SE" and "Footsie" are trade marks of the London Stock Exchange and The Financial Times and are used by FTSE International under licence . † Sector P/E ratios greater than 80 are not shown. For changes to FTSE Fledgling Index constituents please refer to www.ftse.com/indexchanges. ‡ Values are negative.

figure 3.1 Average yield for industry sectors, published each day in the *Financial Times*

Source: *Financial Times*

We shall examine the chart patterns, their significance and meanings as well as how to use them to your advantage in detail in Chapter 6.

At this stage, I want to show you how to recognise when the market has demonstrated that the bear trend is over, and to avoid being sucked into a possible false impression that the recovery has started when the technical signs are contrary.

Let us start with part of the chart of the FTSE 100 share index in 1987 (Figure 3.2). The index had climbed steadily and stood at 2,382 on 28 September 1987. It then dropped almost vertically to a low of 1,579 on 30 November – a loss of 803 points, or 32.97 per cent in two months. You can see from Figure 3.2 that it climbed slowly after an initial rebound from 1,579 to 1,712 by 31 December 1987.

After that, the climb followed the usual oscillating line to closing levels as follows:

31 March	1988	1,742
29 July	1988	1,853
30 December	1988	1,765
30 January	1989	2,069

So it took nearly eighteen months from its previous high of 2,382 to recover 490 points out of the 803 that it had lost.

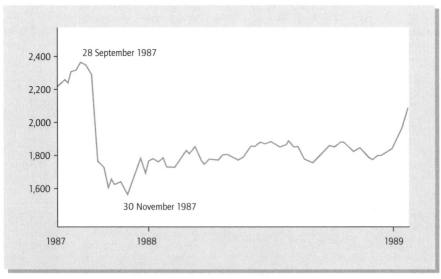

figure 3.2   FTSE 100, August 1987 to February 1989

It never dropped below its 'low' of 1,579, nor did it test that level during the subsequent period of recovery. The recovery was slow, but the trend was always upwards.

Under the present burden of massive debt reduction facing the government, which will inevitably mean higher tax demands on corporate earnings, you should not be surprised if recovery takes substantially longer.

Wait until an upward trend in the FTSE 100 has been established for at least six months.

Summary

In this chapter we explain how you will know when the market has turned by using:

■ Reliable sources of essential data rather than rumour or opinion published by newspapers or TV reporters.

4

Essential tools for fundamental analysis

This chapter describes the essential tools that you need to employ and covers:

- Company reports and accounts.

- The minimum levels the key ratios should reach.

- How to recognise danger signals.

- How the key ratios are calculated.

Company reports and accounts

There are a number of analytical tools that are at the disposal of the private investor. Some, including the way in which company reports and accounts are presented nowadays, have become much more user friendly than they used to be. A standardised and more logical layout has been developed both because of popular demand by the hugely increased size of the investing public, and also because the stock exchange authorities and the Institute of Chartered Accountants have collaborated in designing vastly improved reporting practices to ensure transparency of data presentation to safeguard all investors, whether actual or potential.

The development of computer technology has made access to historical audited data quicker and cheaper so the private investor has the same access to financial information as do the professional fund managers.

Also, the wide availability of information concerning individual share performance and the ability to receive real-time prices gives a serious private investor access to similar tools as the professional, provided the non-professional learns 'the trade' and knows both what signals to look for and how to interpret them. This book is designed to help on both these fronts.

The main sources of these analytical tools are:

- company reports and accounts;
- charts showing a historical record of a company's share price movements.

There are two categories of analysis that investors can employ:

- Fundamental.
- Technical.

Usually, investors adopt one or the other, seldom both. Yet I believe there is a useful role for both categories to play in the analytical research necessary for every investment selected for inclusion in a portfolio, as well as in the mechanisms adopted by private investors to control the downside risks attached to short-term trading. In fact, certain aspects of technical analytical disciplines such as 'point and figure' charts and 'trailing stop-loss limits' are essential weapons in the fight against incurring losses inherent in trading in volatile markets.

I shall describe how to recognise the signals that both fundamental and technical analysis produce, as well as what action you should take to make profits and control losses. Later on, I shall show you how to apply these techniques to investing in a recovering market and at the same time how you should always exercise the greatest possible degree of risk control.

To carry out your fundamental analysis of any company you will need the report and accounts. The latest set of audited accounts for a full year will show you comparative figures for the previous year, so you should obtain the accounts from three years ago. These will include the figures for the year before as well. This will give you the data you need for four consecutive years so that you can see which way the trends are moving in the important ratios. You will also need to study the chart of the share price movement for the past four years at the very least.

To use technical analysis you will need a chart of the share price movement for the past two years only, and you will require access to an up-to-date price feed on your computer. For this, I would suggest ADVFN, which is free, or the TraderPro software from Updata. Daily closing prices will suffice in most cases, but you should not rely on data that is older than that. I shall describe the application and interpretation of technical analysis in the next chapter.

The key ratios that you can get easily from a brief fundamental analysis of the company's accounts are interesting by themselves. They become much more valuable to you when you compare their progress over four or five years.

I want to emphasise that these are figures you would record and compare for the shares that you have selected to hold in your portfolio for long-term growth because they give you an instant picture of the strength or weakness of a company. They also show you whether the company is growing or shrinking, and whether or not the management is efficient in building value for the shareholders.

You should also do these calculations on companies whose shares you are considering buying to hold when the stock market has settled down and become much less volatile, because the pictures that emerge will certainly either confirm your initial positive attitude to the share or warn you against making a possibly expensive mistake.

It doesn't take very long to do them, and with practice you will become adept at ferreting out the relevant data. If you have ten shares that you are keeping long term in your portfolio it will take you about ten minutes per company to get the ratios and write them in a record for each company. You would probably do all of them once a year using the annual report and accounts, and if they issue interim figures also, it will take the same time for those that do so. It is not a great cost to pay for peace of mind.

Fundamental analysis

The main source of the data for fundamental analysis is the company's report and accounts audited by an independent and professional accountant. It is better to use the data shown in the full-year figures, rather than interim reports, although you should monitor these if they are issued to confirm that there has been no major unexpected deviation in the main control ratios or indices since the last year-end results.

Fundamental analysis will enable you to work out several important ratios to tell you about the profit margins of the products, the book value of the shares, the gross profit margins, the stock turnover, and various other key data, but the really important ones for the private investor are these shown below.

- Whether the company is solvent (the quick ratio).
- Whether the company is making enough money to cover its interest liabilities (interest coverage ratio).
- Whether a company has enough working capital.
- The earnings per share (EPS).
- The debt/equity ratio.
- The debt/asset ratio.
- The return on capital employed (ROCE).

By comparing these figures for the last four years at the least, preferably five or seven, you will be able to see immediately whether the company is healthy. If you invest in a company after your initial research, and continue to keep the record, you will be able to make a much more balanced judgement as to whether to hold or sell the investment if the share price has an unexpected fall in the future.

Here are the descriptions of each one together with a guide figure where possible for you to use when deciding whether to continue with your research.

Company solvency ratio (the quick ratio)

$$\text{Quick ratio} = \frac{\text{Current assets}}{\text{Current liabilities}} = \textit{This ratio should never be less than 1}$$

This will tell you whether the company is technically solvent, or not. In this case, the 'solvency' measure depends upon whether or not the current liabilities could be covered by liquid assets if these liabilities had to be repaid immediately. Current liabilities are those debts or charges that will have to be paid within the next twelve months. Current assets are those items for which cash will be received during the same period, plus cash.

There is an important caveat of which you should be aware when you select the constituent parts of 'current assets'. The item 'inventories' or 'stock' will be shown and you can find out in the notes to the accounts whether the value has been arrived at by way of a directors' valuation, or at cost price. You should bear in mind that if the company was forced to liquidate these articles under forced sale conditions, it is most unlikely in most cases that they would get any sum of money near the figure shown. It is worth omitting stock shown from the total of the value of 'current assets' for the purpose of calculating this ratio.

However, you should also bear in mind that companies such as super-markets where the majority of stock is held in foodstuff, either fresh or preserved, will turn over their inventories about every three or four months. When analysing the figures for operators such as these, you should not be alarmed if the ratio is slightly lower than 1:1 if you remove the value of stock or inventory from your calculations.

It is a stringent test, but no decent board of directors should ever allow a situation to arise when they could not demonstrate their ability to cover such a potential crisis should it arise. It is illegal to continue to trade if the company is deemed to be insolvent, and if you ever see this ratio standing at a figure of less than 1:1 you should get out of the share immediately if you hold it, or look for another investment altogether if you are thinking of buying it.

Return on capital employed (ROCE)

This ratio above all others will tell you the most about the management of any company. It will show you:

- How efficient the management has been in building up the value of shareholders' funds.
- Whether any growth in shareholders' funds has beaten the rate of inflation each year.
- How efficient the management has been in changing the company to meet changes in the market for the company's products.
- Whether, under the existing management, the company's days are numbered and you should either not touch the share with a barge pole, or get out quickly if you happen to have the stock in your portfolio.

It is a simple calculation and all you need are the company accounts for the last five years. Most of the constituent members of the FTSE 100 publish their accounts online, so they are easily accessible. If they are not available from the company's web page, you can obtain them from the company secretary, or the finance director, usually without charge, simply by asking for them. You can also get them free from www.advfn.com.

To get the ratios for each accounting period, you add together the issued *ordinary* capital and the reserves (balance sheet). You divide the operating profit (income statement) by the sum of the issued ordinary capital and reserves and multiply by 100.

$$\frac{\text{Issued ordinary capital} + \text{Reserves}}{\text{Operating profit}} \times 100 = \text{ROCE}$$

In the case of Tesco plc the figures are as follows for the year ending 25 February:

	2005	2006	2007	2008	2009
ROCE %	11.8	12.7	12.6	12.9	13.0

This record can be described as solid, but unexciting from an investor's point of view. Although the crash of 2008 occurred in the autumn, and the Tesco year end is 25 February 2009, it is debatable as to what extent sales will have been affected in the last four months of the accounting period. So the verdict on the ability of the management to maintain the momentum upwards, albeit on a gradual slope, must be positive. Certainly it would indicate that management is alert.

If your analysis shows a rising trend for the return on capital employed test, the next item to look at would be the record of the earnings per share for the company.

Earnings per share (EPS)

You arrive at the EPS of a stock by taking the net earnings of the company and dividing them by the number of ordinary shares in issue.

$$\frac{\text{Net earnings}}{\text{Ordinary shares}} = \text{EPS}$$

The reason why it is useful to look at the EPS of a share is mainly for the purpose of comparison with that of another company *in the same sector*.

It would be futile to compare the EPS of a company in the oil industry with that of one in property development, for example. But it is a useful tool when you want to compare 'like with like'. However, bear in mind that the key figures to compare are the numbers of shares in issue. If both companies were making the same amount of net earnings, but one company had ten times the number of ordinary shares in issue, the EPS figure would be very different.

The second point to remember is that the data on which the calculations are based are historical. The net earnings figures can be over eleven months old and much can have happened to the company's fortunes in that time – good or bad.

The same point applies to the current figure shown for return on capital employed (ROCE).

These figures should be looked at for a consecutive period of at least five years so that you can see the trend easily. You are looking for a steadily rising trend of EPS which will confirm the findings for ROCE, or throw up anomalies. This exercise should reinforce your view of the quality of management which you have formed from the ROCE results.

Remember that earnings and dividends are completely different animals:

■ If you see a *dividend* record that is increasing, and an *earnings* record that is declining, there should be some very good reasons for such action. Normally you would react to such a discovery by getting out of the share as fast as possible.

It is worth remembering why people buy shares in the first place, fundamental though it may seem. They buy shares in the expectation that *earnings* will increase. Share prices go up if earnings go up. Simple, yes, but so easily forgotten, as demonstrated by the explosive growth in share prices during the dotcom bubble that began in 1998. People rushed in to buy shares in companies that had only just been formed; which had no trading history whatsoever and which had not even got a product in some cases. There was a 'new philosophy' that was promoted by many investment managers at the time that the payment of dividends restricted the growth of a company, and that the only thing that mattered was product sales. All else would follow from this holy grail. Nobody thought about the costs of achieving these mythical sales, let alone what the net earnings figures might be. But, as so often happens, a collective greed swamped the ordinary investor rather like some sort of emotional pandemic and rational thought and careful analysis were dismissed as old hat. Lots of people lost great sums of money as a result. You only have to look at the chart of the share price of BT to see how disastrous the investment turned out for all those who bought above 350p, and many of those held on to the share after it had turned downwards hoping for a recovery. BT is an established company, with a trading history and profit record and with tangible products found in nearly every home in Britain, and yet its share price collapsed along with the rest of the market sector devoted to telecommunications (Figure 4.1).

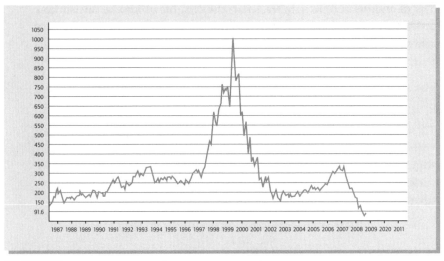

figure 4.1 BT's share price reflected the dotcom boom

Price earnings ratio (PER)

This ratio is very useful when you are comparing the shares of companies *within the same sector* to determine whether the market considers one of them to be better value than the other. Never use it to compare shares from companies in different sectors.

You obtain the PER by expressing the price of a share as a percentage of the earnings per share.

$$\frac{\text{Share price}}{\text{EPS}} \times 100 = \text{PER}$$

The share price is generally taken to mean the price of the ordinary share that is listed on a stock exchange, and the EPS refers to the earnings attributable to the ordinary shares in issue by the company.

The *Financial Times* publishes the PER daily for most of the ordinary shares whose data appears in its columns, and also the FTSE Actuaries Share Indices shows a table wherein the PER is shown for each sector and sub-division within the sectors. An example of the table is shown in Chapter 3 (Figure 3.1).

This very useful tool enables you to see at a glance whether the PER of a company is standing at a level which is above or below the average for the sector and/or its sub-division, as well as letting you compare it directly with that of another company in the same business. Let us look at the banking sector, for example, on 21–22 March 2009 when the extracts in Table 4.1 were taken. The high and low figures cover the last twelve months to that date.

table 4.1 Banking sector summary ratios

Bank	Price (p)	High (p)	Low (p)	Yield (%)	Cover	PER
Barclays	105	510.8	47.3	11.0		4.8
HSBC	371	817.41	270.36	10.6		5.3
LloydsBkg	55.3	488.5	33.0	20.6		2.6
StandCh	895 xd	1,666	554.0	5.6		6.4
Financials	(242)			7.47	1.39	9.61
Banks	(5)			8.51	1.9	6.18

Table 4.1 is useful for several reasons. First, in March 2009, the banks were still reeling from the shocks of 2008, and there was considerable uncertainty as to the extent of the losses incurred by the 'toxic' loans, both from the potential bad debts in the mortgage investments they had made, or acquired, and the value of the many corporate and derivative-based loans outstanding. Their share prices had recovered slightly from the unprecedented low levels that they had reached a few weeks previously.

Second, this picture demonstrates very well an important lesson that is very relevant to all fundamental analyses. Apart from the actual share prices which are current, all the data used to make the calculations such as ratios and dividend cover are historical and can be several months out of date. In Table 4.1, Standard & Chartered's share price is shown as being ex-dividend, so that percentage yield calculation is based on the most recent information of all the companies shown. However, even that is retarded because the ex-dividend period will run for several weeks after the date of the announcement and that announcement will be made several weeks after the end of the accounting period to which the dividend applies.

There is a general perception that as a 'rule of thumb' a high PER means that a share price is expensive relative to its peers, and that a low one means that it is cheap. Very often the answer is not so obvious and much more complicated.

In this example, while the prices of Barclays and Lloyds are certainly relatively cheap, the reason is that they were both out of favour with the market because the threat to their existence posed by so-called toxic debt was much greater than that facing HSBC or Standard & Chartered. The possibility of the need for some provision of extra capital support by the Treasury in one form or another, and perhaps a degree of state control, was deemed to be very real. Such loss of independence, whether wholly or partially, and whether temporally or permanently, would reduce the share price even further. Yet another example of the importance of finding out all the reasons why an anomaly exists when you come across one.

Recent events have shown just how fast market circumstances in general, and individual companies' fortunes in particular, can change. This emphasises the need to look always at a series of such calculations and ratios rather than make decisions based on one set of figures.

So the data shown above gives us the following information.

- Lloyds and Barclays are considered to be the least in demand because their PERs show that they are farthest below the average for the sector, even though their yields are the highest and well above average. The 'price' element (current) in the calculation is clearly very much reduced compared with the 'earnings' element (historical), and so you would be very wary of considering either of these as a long-term investment. Clearly the market expects the yield to fall because the dividends are expected to be lower.

- Depending upon what you discovered in your researches into both these companies, you might buy for recovery, using data based on fundamental analysis. Alternatively you might trade the shares short term using contracts for difference (CFDs) or financial spread betting, until a definite pattern and trend has been established over a period of several months. You should use technical analytical methods to alert you to buy or sell, and most importantly you should impose stop loss levels and calculate potential high and low share price levels.

- If you already owned either of these shares you could use short-term trading methods as an insurance against further loss, particularly to benefit from the dividend if you thought that the historical level might be maintained (unlikely). If a good dividend were to be paid, it would boost the share price substantially.

- If the considerable imbalance between the PERs of Barclays and Lloyds and the other two banks persists, it means that the market has a fairly low opinion of the ability of the management of either of the first two companies to resolve their problems at all quickly.

Thus the immediate conclusion to be drawn from Table 4.1 is that the market considers Barclays and Lloyds to be undervalued, and HSBC and Standard & Chartered to be relatively overvalued. The normal inference being that the market expects the future earnings of HSBC and Standard & Chartered to grow more quickly than those of Barclays and Lloyds, and this is also a reflection of the market's opinion of the level of esteem and confidence in which it holds the management of the four companies. The market is reflecting the opinion of investors, because it is they who are creating a demand for some shares, and increasing the supply for others.

What about the future? Is there any way to anticipate the likely increase in demand or supply of the individual shares?

Price earnings growth, or forward P/E

Many tip sheets and financial analysts often introduce forecasts using figures called forward P/Es to reinforce their argument that the shares of Bloggins & Co are worth buying for capital growth. As we have shown, share price demand grows strongly if there is a widespread belief that earnings will increase substantially in the near term.

The question that you should ask yourself is: 'What are the bases on which these forecasts are made?'

Above-average growth in earnings is needed to achieve an increase in the demand for the shares which will be sufficient to produce above-average growth in the price of the shares.

It is not easy to find published records of growth rates for market sectors, let alone detailed forecasts for future growth rates. Certainly they are not produced in the financial press as are the daily records of prices of shares, government stock, unit trusts and investment trusts. It is perfectly possible to plot the growth rates (or rates of decline) for each individual company from the databases of most of the software provided by stock and share information services, but this is a time-consuming exercise. Also, it is possible sometimes to get some clues about the future order books of certain high-profile companies when they report winning a very large value contract to manufacture or supply a product to a particular customer market for the next year or two. Examples such as British Aerospace winning a contract to supply fighter aircraft to Saudi Arabia, or Rolls-Royce getting an order to manufacture several hundred aircraft engines for the Airbus for some national airlines over the next two or three years might qualify, but these are the exceptions. Usually, any forecasts for the earnings for the next twelve months are made either by the directors or by someone deemed to be an 'expert' in the particular industry.

Such forecasts are subject to the vagaries of unexpected consequences which can so easily render predictions worthless. For example, if a sector has grown at the rate of, say, 10 per cent in the last twelve months, a company's earnings would probably have to grow at least 20 per cent for the next twelve months to establish what might be described as 'above average expansion' to attract the sort of support for the share price needed to create sufficient and extraordinary demand. You should ask yourself whether there is enough evidence (as opposed to opinion) to justify taking on a risk which would certainly be above average since you would be unlikely to be able to corroborate the claims from reliable third-party sources.

Never forget the old stock exchange adage: 'Where there's a tip – there's a tap'.

You will do well to note all such forecasts if they arise about any individual share in which you may be interested, but at the same time maintain your questioning approach until you have sufficient independent evidence from a reputable source to confirm your decision to accept the risks.

Dividend cover

This figure tells you how many times the cost of the dividend paid to the holders of the ordinary shares is covered by the profits generated that are attributable to the ordinary shares in issue. It is a measure of the ability of the management to generate sufficient profits to cover all charges and other costs including loan interest, preference dividends if any, and there should always be a surplus after paying the dividend to the ordinary shareholders to add to reserves and enhance the value of the company.

Generally, you would expect to see a dividend cover of at least 2x, but there are certain categories of company or instrument that are outside this rule. Investment trusts and unit trusts designed for capital growth, exchange-traded commodities, zero dividend preference shares, capital shares, gilts, and venture capital trusts (VCTs) for example. All VCTs are prevented by law from making any distribution for the first five years of their life.

In the current financial climate as the market is starting to recover from the effects of the crash of 2008, you should look for a dividend cover of more than 3x to be safe for any share that you are intending to buy to hold.

You should always beware of investing in any company where you can see that the dividend cover is falling consecutively. It means that the amount of net earnings available for distribution to the ordinary shareholders is becoming progressively less each year. This reduction in net earnings means that either the product sales are falling, or that costs are increasing and profit margins are being squeezed. It is not a good sign. I believe that an early warning sign alerts me when I see so-called cheap offers of a product, or buy-one-get-one-free, known in the retail trade as a BOGOF. I believe it is a sign that the company is losing market share, or that sales volume is falling. Any reduction in product price represents a reduction in profits, which ultimately means a reduction in earnings for the seller.

Interest coverage ratio

This will tell you whether or not a company is generating enough cash flow to cover its annual interest payment liabilities. To calculate the earnings before interest, tax, depreciation and amortisation (EBITDA) you take the net earnings and add back the cost of interest, taxes, depreciation and amortisation and divide this figure by the cost of interest.

$$\text{Interest coverage ratio} = \frac{\text{EBITDA}}{\text{Cost of interest}}$$

The ratio should be 1.5 : 1 or higher. Any ratio less than 1 : 1 means the company is having difficulties in generating enough cash flow to cover its interest liabilities.

Interest cover is very important at the present time because the banks have lost so much money through their accumulation of poor-quality loans, sometimes called toxic assets. They are very much afraid of letting their loan books become vulnerable to any more losses so they will restrict, or sometimes even withdraw credit to their corporate customers if they think that there is any danger of the company not generating enough cash to meet its interest payments as they fall due.

Clearly, should this danger become real for a listed company, particularly one with a very large market capitalisation, and if a warning rumour or adverse press comment were to spread, the share price would suffer badly, as happened with Northern Rock.

Debt control and cash flow

There is no doubt that the two most important items to be watched in any corporate financial analysis that you do for the next few years are debt control and cash flow. These two represent the heart and lungs of a company, and if either of them is stopped or becomes inadequate, the company will fail.

You can get all the information you need to tell you at a glance whether the management of any company you choose has got a grip on these two vital factors by looking at the company financial information data free on www.advfn.com.

Summary

In this chapter we explained why it is so important to monitor the key ratios including:

- Company solvency ratio.

- Return on capital employed.

- Earnings per share.

- Price earnings ratio.

- Price earnings growth.

- Dividend cover.

- Interest coverage ratio.

5

Technical analysis

In this chapter we examine the importance of technical analysis and the signals given by:

- Linear charting;
- Trend lines;
- Support and resistance levels;
- Head and shoulders;
- Reverse head and shoulders;
- MACDs;
- Bollinger bands.

Technical analysis (linear charting)

Technical analysis attracts some adherents who firmly believe that fundamental analysis plays no useful part whatsoever in the art of forecasting the movement of the market price of shares, commodities, or anything else where the trade is volatile. Their argument is based upon the premises that markets are dynamic, and the movement of the constituent parts (e.g. share prices) conform to certain historical patterns of behaviour. The historical movements reveal constraints on the direction of movement of these prices, as well as providing advance signals as to when the movement is about to change direction, and that these patterns will exert similar influences in the future. Some of these constraints are called 'support' and 'resistance' levels. Some are patterns of share price behaviour that are precursors to changes in direction, such as 'head and shoulders', 'double tops', or 'double bottoms'.

The technical analyst is not concerned at all in why anything happened to the share price in the past; only what it is going to do in the future.

There is merit in both types of analysis and I am convinced that they both have a useful part to play in the tool box of the private investor.

Why look at historical data?

There are two main objectives for any investor:

- To build a portfolio (whether it is for growth or income, or both) tailored to your own particular requirements.
- To maximise short-term capital gains in addition to the performance produced by your long-term portfolio. Also, possibly to create some temporary 'insurance' against potential loss that has been identified in one of the constituents of your portfolio.

You really do need to analyse historical data over several years when researching what to buy to hold in a portfolio, since the objective is to invest your capital so that it grows at a rate above annual inflation and to reduce the costs of buying and selling as much as possible. Identifying price behaviour patterns of individual shares will arm you with knowledge and enable you to control your risks, as well as giving you realistic profit targets.

Also, technical analysis is the most efficient tool to employ, particularly when contemplating short-term trading to obtain capital gain, providing the profit generated exceeds the cost of buying and selling and stamp duty and interest charges.

What types of chart presentation should I use?

The source for technical analysis that you will need is a daily chart of the individual share price of each company or index. The type of chart most commonly used is a linear chart. Such chart presentations are easy to understand, and most people feel comfortable with them.

There is only one disadvantage to using linear charts for all your analyses and risk control mechanisms. They show every single movement of the share price, both up and down, however small. For various reasons, which are explained in much greater detail in the next chapter, you will find it much easier to recognise the signals that this technique illuminates, particularly in helping you to make buy or sell decisions. It is not difficult to learn how to use and read this type of chart and by so doing you will enhance your performance and increase your profits considerably.

The following patterns or signals using linear charts are the ones most commonly used, and they are very easy to apply and understand. These are all demonstrated using linear charts.

Trend

Trend lines *must* be parallel. They are drawn with one line linking the 'tops' or peaks of a share price record and a parallel line linking the 'bottoms' or troughs. Trend lines tell you two facts. They define the top and bottom limits of the current trading range that is enclosed between the two parallel lines, and they show you at a glance whether the overall direction of the trading range is trending up, down, or horizontally. During any period, the limits defined by the trend lines become the top and bottom values between which the share price moved, in both an upward and downward direction. Thus, during that period, when it changed direction you would expect that the price would not exceed the limits, either top or bottom, that were indicated by the trend lines.

In the example of the share price of Pearson plc (Figure 5.1), you can see how the share price oscillates between the parallel lines from October 2008 to May 2009. The trend is upwards during this period, and the price has risen from 520p to about 720p. This represents a growth of 200p, or almost 40 per cent in seven months. If you had bought the share at a price of, say, 550p and sold it at, say, 700p, which is more likely if you had been following the signals that I describe hereunder, you would have shown a profit of about 150p (before dealing costs and stamp duty) or over 27 per cent.

The annual rate of increase in the price as shown by the trend lines was there to be measured, and you could see examples of trends having been

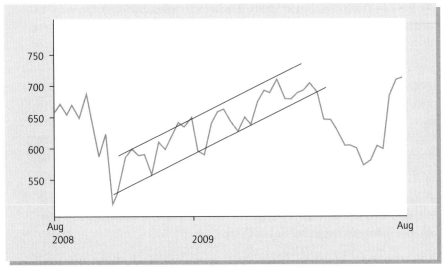

figure 5.1 Pearson share price shows upward trend

established historically, both upwards and downwards, which gave you an indication of the percentage rise and fall that you could reasonably expect over measurable periods of time.

As the days progressed, when the price had broken out from within the parallel lines, you would have had to wait until it was obvious that a new trend and direction had become established before you could start to make new predictions with any degree of certainty as to how far the price might rise or fall and whether the trend had changed direction.

Lines of resistance/Support levels

Lines of resistance and support are always horizontal, and you establish them by drawing a line across the chart connecting up the peaks and troughs in the same way that you connected them to establish a trend.

The best way to think of lines of resistance or support is to think of floors and ceilings, and a bouncing ball. When the price line falls to a level and turns upwards, it is said to have hit a support. If it returns again to the same level and turns upward again, it is said to confirm a support. The more times it hits the support level and bounces back up from that price, the stronger the support is considered to be. In this instance the price is the ball, and the support level becomes the floor.

As we have seen, the price will be a direct reflection of the supply or demand function so that you can assume that when it falls to a certain level, buyers consider the share price to be good value and they become active, thereby turning 'supply' into 'demand'.

In the same way, if the share price (ball) pierces the support level (floor) and drops to a new low, there will come a time when it will establish a new 'floor'. Very often when it has broken through the floor and fallen sufficiently far, the old floor becomes the new 'ceiling'. If it starts to climb back after this latest drop, you need to see if it penetrates the new ceiling, or bounces back off the new ceiling and moves back down to the new floor.

When a share price establishes a new ceiling and floor, it is said to have formed a new trading range.

The trading range can be described as the difference between two price levels, top and bottom. The trading range can be demonstrated by parallel lines either trending horizontally as in Figire 5.2, or upwards as in Figure 5.1 or downwards as in Figure 5.3.

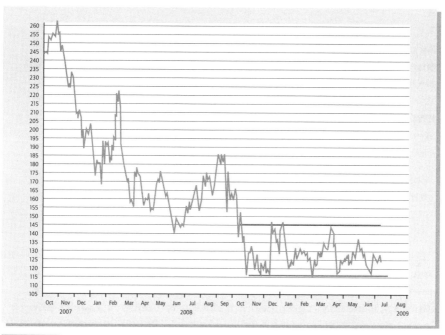

figure 5.2 **Filtrona share price oscillates between two horizontal boundaries**

Source: Updata plc

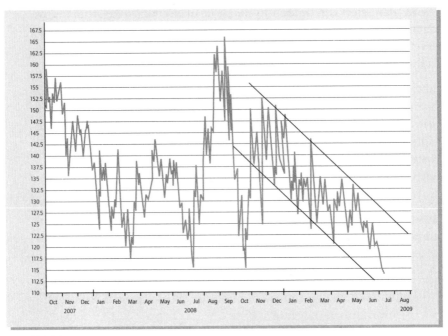

figure 5.3 RSA share price shows downward trend for the trading range

For short-term trading, the direction of the trading range does not matter. You have the option to trade short-term for capital growth either by buying or selling short anyway, so you can make money on a falling price as well as on a rising one. Its main benefit to you is to demonstrate the likely price levels at which you can expect the price movement to turn against your selected position so you know when to close out your position to reduce the risk of making a loss.

There are two important points to bear in mind when you are contemplating trading a share in the short term.

First, when the share price has established its trading range, and you have decided to let the momentum of the price movement boost your potential earnings that you hope to win in this trade, wait before you open your 'buy' or 'sell' position until the price has gone as far as it is going to rise or fall within the trading range parameters *and turned and established its new direction* before you give the order. This will safeguard your capital just in case the price does not turn, but continues in its current direction of movement and breaks out from the trading range. A good example of how to anticipate the potential influence of resistance and support levels and trend parameters can be seen in the chart of Bellway in Figure 5.4. This shows a rising trend, and at the same time different resistance and support levels. The resistance and support levels are marked 1, 2, and 3. The trend lines are marked AA, top and bottom.

The share price then breaks downwards through the upwards trend line. If it turns upwards when it reaches the 600p level (resistance level 1), then the next level for it to breach will be level 2 at 650p. On the other hand, if it breaks through level 1 continuing downwards, the next level for it to test would be around 525p. You should wait to see which way it moves after it has reached level 1 (600p).

Second, it does not matter whether you decide to 'buy' or 'sell' after you have taken every precaution to confirm the new direction of price movement – *impose a stop-loss* in the opposite direction. I shall describe this insurance policy and how best to reinforce your risk control later on in the book. I cannot stress strongly enough how important it is to get into the habit automatically of applying a stop-loss limit when you are trading short term.

figure 5.4   Bellway share price with trend lines (AA) and resistance and support
levels (1–3)   Source: Updata plc

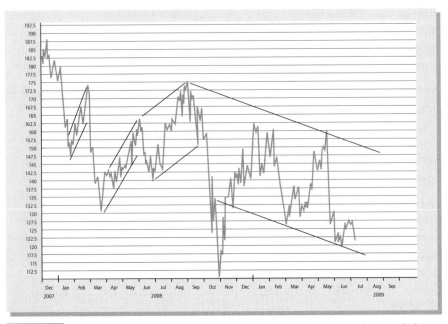

figure 5.5   Cable & Wireless shows varying trading ranges and the price trend alters direction

Source: Updata plc

You can see from the chart shown as Figure 5.5 that there were occasions in the past two years when the Cable & Wireless share price trend altered direction, and different trading ranges were formed. Yet again, I want to stress the need to look back at any trading history as far as possible to start with, because you will get a much better feel for the behaviour pattern of the share price. You will be able to get a sense also of how much the share price reacted in the past to any major factors, whether national or international that affected the sector or the market as a whole, such as interest rate or oil price changes, the dotcom bubble, war, or some other force majeure. The lessons that you can learn from this history include a very important one. It shows how easy it is to lose money if you jump to a conclusion too quickly about the establishment of a new trading range, or a definite change in the direction of the trend, too soon after the share price has broken out from its established parameters.

You will see occasions also when the share price penetrates the floor or ceiling of its trading range, but then returns very quickly back into the previous limits without establishing any new direction or price range. Thus, while it is good advice to close out a trading position quickly when a share price breaks out so that you limit as much potential loss as possible, the outcome of eliminating any further risk may penalise you from profiting from further gain which you might have won if you had kept the position open. Better safe than sorry.

Double tops

When you see a double top forming in a linear chart, and even more so when you occasionally see a triple-top configuration, it means that the share price is about to fall (Figure 5.6).

It is a forceful demonstration of a share price bouncing off a ceiling, and very often it occurs because there is a substantial amount of profit taking by investors who have bought at much lower price levels. Demand turning into supply.

There is only one proviso for this substantial change in direction to be a virtual certainty, and that is that the tops should occur several weeks apart. As a rule of thumb the interval is generally taken to be four or five weeks, but it is a very strong signal.

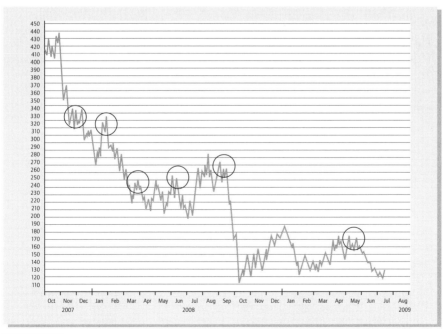

figure 5.6   **British Airways shows double tops come before a fall**   Source: Updata plc

Double bottom

A double bottom is a very strong signal that the price movement is about to rise (Figure 5.7). We explained earlier that a strong resistance level will convert supply into demand when a large enough number of investors consider a certain price level to represent above average value and follow up their conviction with purchase action. In fact, a case could easily be made for restricting your dealing to occasions only when these signals occur, and dealing in substantial sums when they do.

You can see several instances in the example given in Figures 5.6 and 5.7 which illustrate very well how often double tops and bottoms occurred in the history of the share price of British Airways over an eighteen-month period.

Head and shoulders

Both the chart patterns head and shoulders, and the opposite, reverse head and shoulders, are significant for two reasons. In both cases they

figure 5.7 British Airways shows double bottoms preceding price rises   Source: Updata plc

signal a forthcoming change of direction in the price movement. They also give you a good idea of the probable distance the price will rise or fall. They both represent good opportunities to make profits in a short time, and offer low-risk situations in which the professional traders will invest larger amounts of capital than they would normally.

You can see from the chart of Rio Tinto (Figure 5.8) that in May 2008 a head and shoulders pattern occurred and the price rose from a 'shoulder' of about 6,500p to a 'head' of about 7,200p, or by around 700p. It then fell in a few days from the second 'shoulder' almost in a straight line to a low of 6,100p, or a fall of around 500p.

Normally, you should expect the reaction from a head and shoulders pattern to be at least the same amount as the increase in share price measured between the shoulders and the head. Often it is greater, as shown in this example. Also, you should expect the price to fall either at the same speed, or a very much shorter space of time measured from the second shoulder, than the time taken for it to rise from the first shoulder.

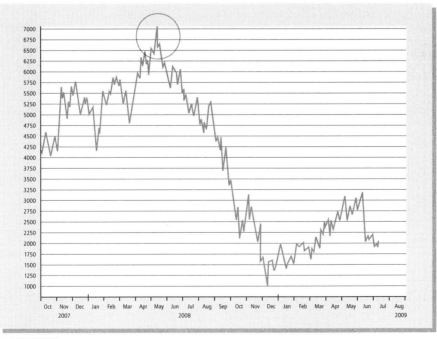

figure 5.8 **Head and shoulders demonstrated by Rio Tinto**   Source: Updata plc

You will be able to get a good idea of the time that you should expect to elapse from when the price turns down at the second shoulder to the bottom of the drop both by looking at previous resistance levels and extrapolating them as I have explained above.

A reverse head and shoulders pattern (Figure 5.9) will give as strong a signal as a head and shoulders, and offer the same excellent opportunity to make good profits. You can expect to see all the same degrees of measurements in the price movements, and at the same speeds, but simply operating in reverse.

Whereas you would 'short sell' the share when you see a head and shoulders pattern forming, you 'buy' the share, or place an up-bet when you see a reverse head and shoulders pattern starting to appear.

Either way, these two signals are very good news for trading, and it is worth regularly trawling through as many charts as you can just looking for signs that they are emerging in any share price current record, whether you hold the share in a portfolio, or perhaps might be interested in the share in the future depending upon its future performance, or have no other interest in it whatsoever.

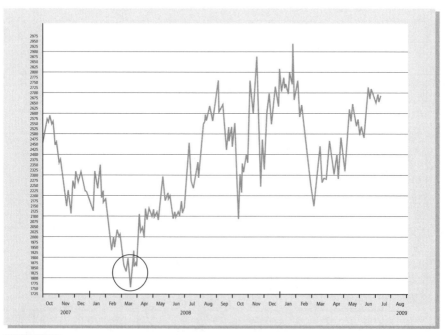

figure 5.9   **Reverse head and shoulders in March 2008 for AstraZeneca**   Source: Updata plc

Chart momentum

You can get a good idea of the 'chart momentum' by looking at the historic share price picture shown on the chart over a period of, say, two years. As a simplification, if the share price has risen and fallen substantially and consistently over that time, you can expect this more rapid oscillation to continue. It clearly demonstrates there is a great deal of trade taking place in the share and that sentiment changes quickly in either direction. This sort of regular volatility over a relatively short period is exactly what a short-term trader looks for as a potentially profitable vehicle to use both on the way up, and on the way down.

The price history of British American Tobacco illustrates this case in point (Figure 5.10). You can see most of the signals that I have described occurring regularly and the rise and fall in money terms on most occasions is substantial. This is a share that should be watched all the time to take advantage of profitable opportunities in the share price movement and it certainly would require the judicious use of trailing stop-loss limits, which I shall describe later on in the book in the section covering risk control.

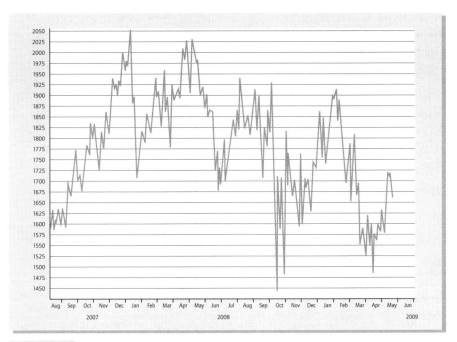

figure 5.10 British American Tobacco should be watched for the regular opportunities it throws up

Source: Updata plc

Moving average convergence/divergence (MACD)

Moving average convergence/divergence, known as MACD, is a technical analysis indicator and it is a very useful tool. Its main claim to fame is as an advance warning indicator to alert you to an imminent change in the direction of a share price. It is very useful for short-term trading using either CFDs or spread betting. It will alert you to an opportunity to buy or place an up-bet, or to sell short or close out an up-bet and place a down-bet.

It consists of the differences between two exponential moving averages (EMA) of a share price, one fast and the other slow. The reason why this combination is effective is because it tends to smooth out very short sharp fluctuations, which can give confusing signals. The normal periods that are selected for this control are an EMA of 12 days of price minus an EMA of 26 days of price.

An EMA is calculated by adding together each daily closing price for a period, say 12 days, and dividing the total by 12 to give the moving average. On the thirteenth day, the closing price for that day is added to the previous total, and the closing price for the first day is subtracted. The new 12-day total is then divided by 12 and the new moving average is found. The same exercise is carried out with 26-day totals, adding and subtracting in the same way to produce the 26-day moving average. See the example for HSBC in Figure 5.11.

The MACD (the difference between the two EMAs) is plotted together with one more EMA, usually called the signal line. This EMA is calculated in exactly the same way as the 12-day and 26-day periods of closing price moving averages, but the period that is most widely used for the signal line is a 9-day moving average.

The most useful trading signals that this valuable indicator produces are:

- The MACD line crossing the signal line.
- The MACD line crossing 0.

It is useful to compare the MACD chart with the actual price chart and you will soon understand the relationships between the two main lines, as well as being able to interpret the signals more accurately.

A crossing of the MACD line up through the zero line on the chart is considered to be a bullish crossover, whereas if it crosses downwards through the zero line it is considered to be a bearish crossover.

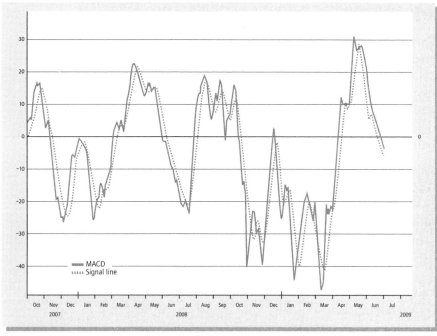

figure 5.11 Moving average plot for HSBC

Source: Updata plc

There will be occasions when there is divergence between the MACD line and the price line. This will happen when, for instance, the share price makes a new 'low' but the MACD does *not* make a new low. It remains above where it fell to when the share price hit the same low level previously. This is interpreted as bullish and suggests that the down trend may be nearly over. There will also be occasions when the opposite occurs. It can happen when the share price makes a new 'high' but the MACD does not rise to the same height as it did on a previous occasion when the share price hit the same high level. This is interpreted as bearish.

You can employ a safety device to ensure that the crossover signal given (indicating a change in the share price trend) is established. For example, you might impose a discipline on yourself that forbids you to *buy to open* a position for three days after the MACD line breaks upwards above the 9-day signal line, and remains above it for three days at which point you place your order. The same discipline could be imposed in reverse if the MACD line cuts down through the 9-day signal line and you delay placing a *sell to open* instruction. However, if you have an open position already and the change in direction signal occurs, *you should not wait to close it*.

Bollinger bands

This device is designed to demonstrate the degree of volatility in a share price. It is *not* intended to give buy or sell signals, but it can be an aid to decision making. The Bollinger band is based on a simple concept. It is that share prices, whilst trending upwards or downwards, always move on an erratic path. If you plot the average price line, and the share price keeps deviating up and down across the track of the 'average', it will keep returning to the average price during its next dart upwards or downwards.

The theory is that the picture shows you whether the share price is over-valued or undervalued i.e. overbought or oversold.

The normal 'average' is based on a 21-day moving average, with the upper and lower bands being anything between 3.5 per cent to 4 per cent higher and lower than the moving average.

You do not have to wait until the price line touches the outer bands before you invest, but I believe that it is best to wait until the share price has turned and only then commit your capital to risk. It should be used in conjunction with point and figure charts (Chapter 6).

figure 5.12   **Bollinger bands for Severn Trent**   Source: Updata plc

When the outer bands are wide apart from the moving average line, it denotes strong volatility, which is what a trader is looking for. When they are close together, ignore the share and look for another.

Note in Figure 5.12 how the outer bands are moving strongly apart.

Summary

In this chapter we demonstrated the use in forecasting future share price movements and the importance of:

■ Trend lines.

■ Resistance and support levels.

■ Head and shoulders.

■ Reverse head and shoulders.

■ Double tops.

■ Double bottoms.

■ MACD.

■ Bollinger bands.

Point and figure charting

In this chapter we show you how to construct a point and figure chart, including:

- Box size;

- Box reversal;

- The reasons why Xs and Os are kept separate;

- The signals the charts give you;

- Support and resistance levels.

Technical analysis (point and figure charting)

At first sight, a point and figure chart looks nothing like a linear chart. Because the natural tendency is to treat anything we don't understand with suspicion, and keep it at arm's length, we tend not to embrace point and figure charting as enthusiastically as we should. But it is one of the most useful and valuable tools available to a trader or investor and it will pay you dividends many times over for the small amount of time it takes to learn how to use it.

It looks completely different from a linear chart. There is a very good reason why, and this is one of its great strengths.

A linear chart presents a record of a share price, *whether there is any change in the price or not.* If there is no trade in the share for an hour, or a day, or a week, the linear chart will simply show a straight line during the period. If there are small changes in the price; up a bit, down a bit, some erratic movements over a period, a linear chart will record all of these. Professional traders call this incidental and unimportant oscillation 'chatter' or 'noise'. It really is not important to the investor. A point and figure chart will not react unless there is a significant change in the price. If not enough is happening, the chart will not move.

How are they constructed?

The characteristics of point and figure charts must be understood if you are going to be able to get the maximum benefit from interpreting them and using the tool to maximise your profits and reduce your exposure to risk as far as possible.

These are the unique features of a point and figure chart:

- Normally they use an X or an O instead of lines or bars.
- An X represents a sequential movement *up* in price.
- An O represents a sequential movement *down* in price.
- Xs and Os are called 'boxes'.
- Each X and O represents a variable pre-selected price amount which is called 'box size'.
- Price changes of amounts less than the box size are ignored when plotting the chart.
- A column of Xs changes to a column of Os (and vice versa) when the price changes direction by a pre-selected number of boxes. This is called the 'reversal size'.
- The columns of Xs and Os represent demand (buying) and supply (selling).
- The chart sensitivity can be varied to show the short, medium and long-term position using the same data.
- No record is made of price gaps.
- Price is scaled on the vertical y axis.
- There is no time-scale on the horizontal x axis.
- Time plays no part in the construction of point and figure charts.

- Although there is no time axis, point and figure charts are two-dimensional charts.
- Point and figure charts are named according to their box and reversal size.

Up moves and down moves

An X is used for an upward move in the price and an O is used for a downward move in the price. You never put an X or an O in the same vertical column.

This makes it very easy to see the general trend, and it also shows clearly the overall upward and downward movement within the trading range.

Box size

This element is one of the points of difference between point and figure charts and any others. When the chart is being constructed, you decide on the 'value' of the box size. It could be one point, half a point, five, ten, fifty or another number of points.

Whatever the number of points you designate for any given share or index, no X box or O box may be plotted until the price has risen or fallen by that amount. Thus, if you have given the box size a figure of 20 points, and the price rose 19 points (or pence, or cents, or whatever denomination you are using), you would not plot the next X box above the existing one because the price had not risen by sufficient value. The same rule would apply in reverse. You would not plot the next O box below the existing one until the price had fallen by at least 20 points.

The reason why you designate different values to a box is because you can use point and figure charting for any instrument that is traded. For example, you would probably use a 50-point box size for the FTSE 100 index, and a 15-point box size for Imperial Tobacco group (1608p).

The box represents the price, not the line.

With a linear chart, the price levels are represented by horizontal lines marked on the Y (vertical) axis. Thus you can see when the price reached a level of, say, 100 because the price line meets the 100 line on the chart and you can see when the line reached, surpassed or fell below it. Point and figure charts will simply show an X or an O above or below the 100 line, with no indication of when the price reached this level.

Box reversal size

The reversal size is an important part of point and figure chart construction. It is the number of boxes required to change your plot from a column of Xs (rising price run) to a column of Os (falling price run), or vice versa.

It is possible to use a one-box, three-box, or five-box reversal factor, but the normal practice is to use a three-box reversal. This means that the price has to change direction by the minimum amount of three times the box value before you change your plot from X to O, or vice versa.

Gaps

Point and figure charts do not record gaps in a price history. If the price jumps from 10 to 15, each price is recorded between the two numbers by an X (box size being the determining factor as to how many of the numbers are included). The same applies for a price fall.

Time

Point and figure charts do not record time. Unlike other charts, time is of no importance. They only record price movement.

Signal strength

Because all price rises are marked by an X, and all price falls are marked with an O, and since all the Xs and Os are kept in separate vertical columns until there is a change in direction of the movement of the price, it is easy to see quickly whether a rise or fall was relatively normal (within the trading range and thus to be expected), or strong and protracted. You can see this difference at a glance simply by noting the length of the column of Xs or Os, and with practice it will become automatic.

Box reversal

Sometimes the number of boxes chosen to be used when the price changes direction may be one, three or five. The number most frequently used is three. I shall only explain the construction of a three-box reversal technique, and only give examples in this book using it.

I strongly recommend the best and most easily understood work on this whole technique, which is *The Definitive Guide to Point and Figure* by

Jeremy du Plessis (Harriman House Publishing) where the subject is explained in considerable depth by the leading expert in Britain.

At the top of every point and figure chart there is a legend that tells you the name of the company or index, the number of points or pence or cents that each box represents, as well as the number of boxes used for the reversal in that chart. It should include the code name as well. For example, Dow Jones (INDU) Daily P&F (closing price) 100 × 3. This translates as: the Dow Jones Industrial Index; Code INDU; Point and Figure chart; plotting daily closing prices; box size 100 points; three-box reversal size.

Point and figure chart construction

There are three points that it is essential to remember:

1 When using a three-box reversal construction for a point and figure chart you never mix Xs and Os in the same column. It is permissible to do this in a one-box reversal chart, but I shall only be explaining the use of a three-box reversal.

2 Whatever value in points or money you assign to a box for an individual stock, share, index or commodity, the same value applies whether the movement is up (X) or down (O).

3 When the price reverses (changes direction from upwards to downwards, or vice versa), when you start the next column you always begin with the first X or O on the next level up, or down from the last entry in the previous column as in Figure 6.1.

From Figure 6.1 you can see that the first plot was in column number 1. For illustrative purposes I have shown this X in bold. Since we are learning how a three-box reversal chart is constructed, remember that the first box plotted in a new column consists of three units. Let us assume that the units in this case are 10p, and consequently for the plot to start in a new column, whether Xs or Os, the price must have moved up or down by at least 30p (3 × 10p = 30p).

Assume that the price started by rising from 50p to 70p (up 30p) from a previous column which turned when the price had reached 40p. In this example, the plot starts with the price moving upwards, so you would put three Xs in the column.

Assume that the price moved up at least another 10p. Not less than 10p.

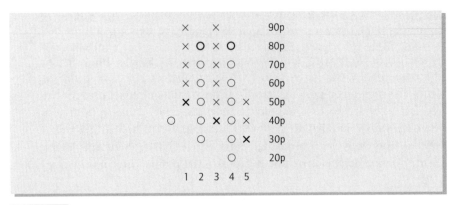

figure 6.1   A point and figure chart

It moves to the 90p level, or 90p + (so long as it does not reach more than 99p). You plot another two Xs in the same column. The price now turns downward. It must fall by at least 30p ($3 \times 10p = 30p$) for the three-box reversal to be activated.

It must fall by at least 30p from the last box plotted, the actual price is immaterial.

In this case, it must fall to 60p minimum (but not to lower than 59p). Let us assume it falls to 60p. You always plot the first mark (O) in a new column one level below the last mark (X) in the previous column if the reversal has turned into a downward direction, and you always plot the first mark (X) in a new column one level above the last mark (O) in the previous column if the reversal has turned into an upward direction.

Again for illustrative purposes I have shown the first mark in each column demonstrating a reversal in bold. In this reversal from an upward movement to a downward direction it is shown as **O**.

The price having fallen from 90p to 60p, you plot three Os starting with the first one at the 80p level. The price has moved down 90p to 80p, 80p to 70p, 70p to 60p. So you plot an O at each level to 60p, starting with the first level in column 2 below the level of the last X, which was plotted at 90p.

The price continues to fall and for every complete 10p that it falls below the mark at which it was last plotted you mark an O in the same vertical column.

There must not be any gaps in a line of Xs or Os in a vertical column. Unmarked spaces above or below the marks do not matter. They are showing you that the price was rising or falling within the pre-selected limits of the box size (or contents), and because we are using a three-box reversal technique, any small oscillations that occur but which do not exceed three times the box size are ignored. *The reason is that you are only interested in knowing when a change of direction in the price movement has become sufficiently established to become significant.*

Now let us start by examining a typical historical record of a price movement and show you how the point and figure plot would be constructed.

table 6.1		Price movement in pence (starting from 400)								
1.	432	a	11.	491	k	21.	527	u
2.	441	b	12.	505	l	22.	496	v
3.	451	c	13.	554	m	23.	489	w
4.	418	d	14.	518	n	24.	474	x
5.	450	e	15.	488	o	25.	503	y
6.	483	f	16.	504	p	26.	419	z
7.	449	g	17.	525	q	27.	442	α
8.	504	h	18.	531	r	28.	417	β
9.	489	i	19.	563	s	29.	476	γ
10.	499	j	20.	538	t	30.	493	δ

The price range runs from 400 to 570 on the linear chart. So let us construct a point and figure chart using the data shown in Table 6.1 and compare it with the linear chart (Figure 6.2). The construction is shown here step by step so that you can see exactly how it emerges from the record of price movements.

Modern technology enables you to have all this work done for you instantly and delivered to your computer, but it is most important that you understand both what is done and why, if you are to benefit from the signals that point and figure charts produce.

Consider the price movements one at a time:

▪ The first movement (a) is a rise in price from 400p to 432p, and we shall assume that it comes after a previous fall in price. This rise represents a three-box reversal and so the first entry on the chart is three Xs marked at levels 410p, 420p and 430p (Figure 6.3).

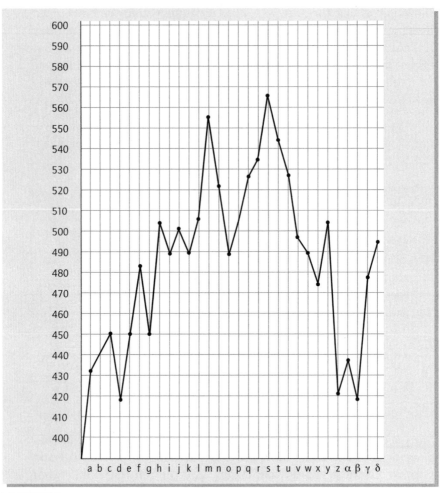

figure 6.2 Linear chart of price movements from Table 6.1

■ The second move is a rise to 441p. You are looking for either a 10p rise from the last level plotted, or a 30p fall from the same level (which would mark a three-box reversal). This rise is more than 10p (being the contents of one full box) so you plot another X in the chart at the 440p mark (Figure 6.4).

Note: You always take the 'price' level of the last plotted box when you are calculating whether to fill the next box, or change columns. Do not make the mistake of using the last price to calculate whether there has been a large enough movement either upwards or downwards to warrant another box or

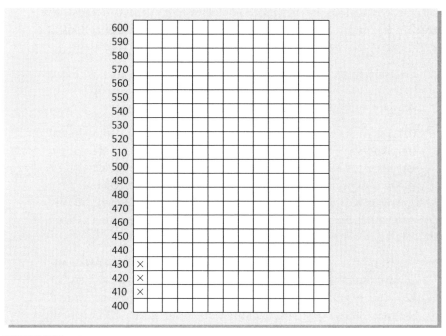

figure 6.3   First entry

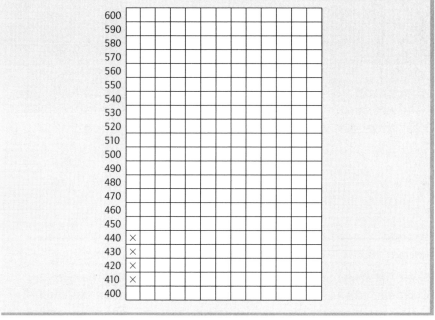

figure 6.4   Second entry

reversal. Once a price has been used to plot an X or O, the actual price level reached is discarded and no record is kept. It is not possible to look at a point and figure chart and know what price generated an X or an O.

■ The third move (c) is a further rise to 451p. The last entry on the chart was at 440p, and since the price has reached the 450p level, you plot another X in that slot (Figure 6.5).

■ The fourth price move (d) is a fall to 418p. The last box plotted was 450p and since the price has turned downwards and we are using a three-box reversal technique, you need to see a fall of at least 30p (3 × 10p = 30p) from the last box plotted to establish a reversal downwards. In this case the price needs to drop to 420p at the very least. It has dropped to 418p, so you plot 3 × O in the next vertical column at the levels 440p, 430p and 420p (Figure 6.6).

■ The fifth price move (e) is another reversal, from downwards to an upward direction. The price rises from 418p to 450p, an increase of 32p. This is sufficient for the three-box reversal requirement of not less than 30p so you plot Xs in the slots in the next vertical column at 430p, 440p and 450p (Figure 6.7).

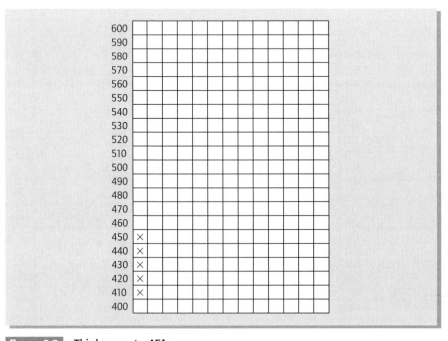

figure 6.5 Third move, to 451p

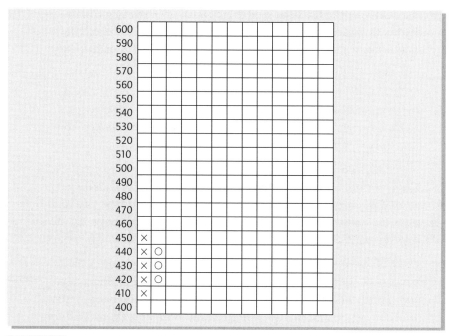

figure 6.6 Price drop of 32p triggers a reversal

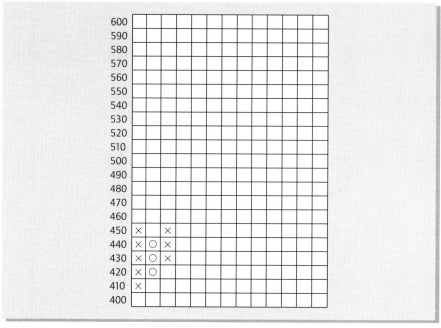

figure 6.7 Another reversal, this time upwards

▓ The price continues to rise (f) and moves on upwards to 483p. The last X was plotted at 450p, so you are looking for a level of not less than 460p or higher in multiples of 10p for each additional X. 483p − 450p = 33p so you add Xs in the same vertical column at the levels of 460p, 470p and 480p (Figure 6.8).

▓ The price reverses (g) and drops from 483p down to 449p, giving a decrease in value of 34p, which is sufficient to fill three boxes. You place three Os in the next vertical column in the slots marked 470p, 460p and 450p (Figure 6.9).

▓ Again, the price reverses and rises from 449p to 504p (h). You are looking for a minimum price rise of 30p from the last box plotted at 450p, i.e. 480p. The rise from 450p to 504p is an increase of 54p. You plot five Xs in the next vertical column at the levels of 460p, 470p, 480p, 490p and 500p (Figure 6.10).

▓ The price drops from 504p to 489p (i). Since this is another change in direction, you are looking for a minimum fall in the price of 30p from the last box plotted at 500p to a minimum of 470p to confirm a three-box reversal. The reduction amounts to 11p only (500p − 489p

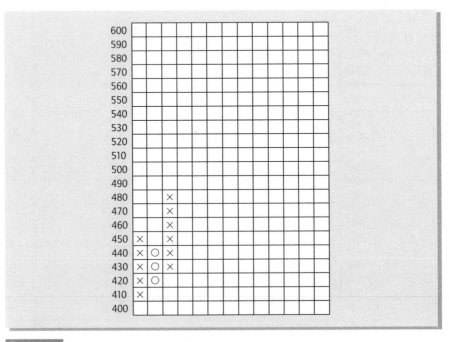

figure 6.8

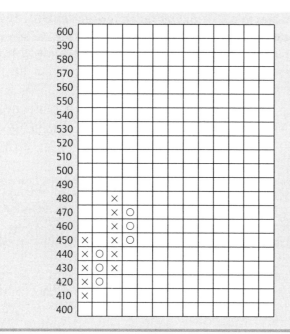

figure 6.9

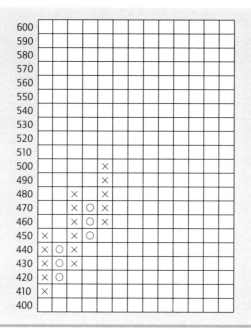

figure 6.10

= 11p). Notice how you measure the amount of the drop by measuring it against the last box plotted, not from the level it reached before. *You ignore the move and wait to see whether the price continues to fall, or changes direction, or remains static.*

■ The price rises (j); from 489p to 499p. The last box plotted was at 500p with an X showing an upward trend. The next price you need to see to continue the upward trend is not less than 510p, or 470p to meet the requirements of a three-box reversal. The rise to 499 does not satisfy either criterion. *You do nothing.*

■ The price drops to 491p (k). The same criteria still apply as described in (j) above. *You do nothing.*

■ The price turns again (l) and rises to 505p. Still not sufficient to continue with another X in the same column as the last mark. *You do nothing.*

■ The price continues upwards to 554p (m). This represents an increase of 54 pence from the last X mark at 500p. You plot five boxes in the same column at the levels 510p, 520p, 530p, 540p and 550p (Figure 6.11).

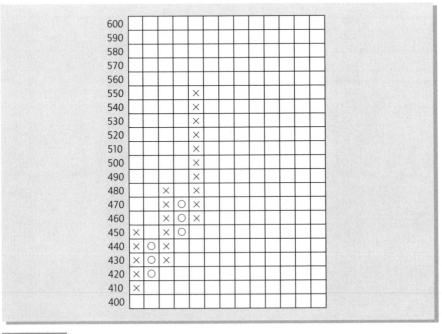

figure 6.11

■ The price now reverses from 554p to 518p (n), or a fall of 36p. The last box plotted was at 550p, so a three-box reversal requires a drop in value of not less than 30p. This fall of 36p enables you to start the next vertical column and plot three Os at the levels 540p, 530p and 520p (Figure 6.12).

■ The price continues to fall (o) and reaches 488p, which is 30p below the last filled box marked at the 520p level. You continue to place Os in the same column at the price levels 510p, 500p, and 490p (Figure 6.13).

■ Now the price turns upwards (p) and rises to 504p, a reversal of 14p from the last box filled. Not enough for a three-box reversal, which needs a climb to not less than 520p. *You do nothing.*

■ The price continues to rise (q) and reaches 525p. This represents an increase from 490p of 35p. You plot three Xs in the next vertical column at the price levels 500p, 510p, and 520p (Figure 6.14).

■ The price continues to rise (r) and reaches 531p. This is an increase of 11p from the last box filled at 520p. You fill in another complete box at the 530 price level (Figure 6.15).

600														
590														
580														
570														
560														
550				×										
540				×	O									
530				×	O									
520				×	O									
510				×										
500				×										
490				×										
480			×	×										
470			×	O	×									
460			×	O	×									
450	×		×	O										
440	×	O	×											
430	×	O	×											
420	×	O												
410	×													
400														

figure 6.12

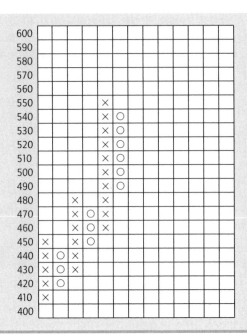

figure 6.13

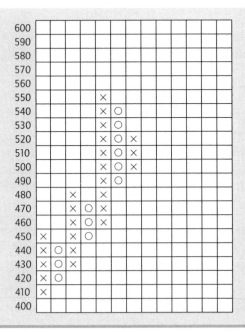

figure 6.14

Price							
600							
590							
580							
570							
560							
550					X		
540					X	O	
530					X	O	X
520					X	O	X
510					X	O	X
500					X	O	X
490					X	O	
480			X		X		
470			X	O	X		
460			X	O	X		
450	X		X	O			
440	X	O	X				
430	X	O	X				
420	X	O					
410	X						
400							

figure 6.15

■ The price goes on up (s) to 563p, which is an increase of 33p above the last box filled. Put Xs in the price levels at 540p, 550p, and 560p in the same column as the last marks (Figure 6.16).

■ The price falls (t) straight down to 538p from 563p. This is a drop of 22p only from the last box mark of 560p, which is not enough to trigger a three-box reversal. *Do nothing.*

■ The fall continues (u) to 527p. This level represents a total drop of 33p from the last full box plotted at 560p. Move to the next vertical column and put Os in the price levels 550p, 540p, and 530p (Figure 6.17).

■ The fall goes on (v) down to 496p, which is 34p lower than the last box plotted at 530p. Put three more Os in the price levels at 520p, 510p, and 500p in the same column (Figure 6.18).

■ The price falls again (w) to 489p. This is only 11p lower than the last full box plotted. *Do nothing.*

■ The price continues downwards (x) to 474p. Since this level is 26p lower than the last box marked in this column at 500p, you plot

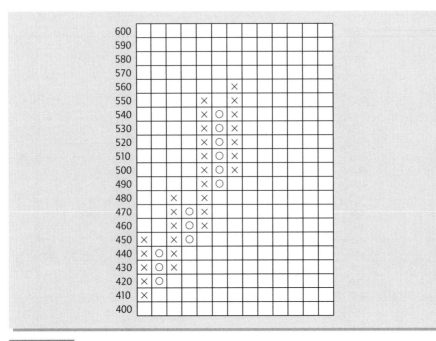

figure 6.16

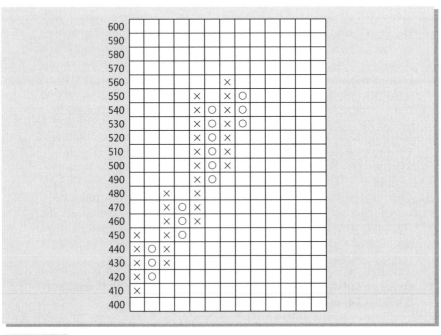

figure 6.17

	1	2	3	4	5	6	7	8					
600													
590													
580													
570													
560							X						
550					X		X	O					
540					X	O	X	O					
530					X	O	X	O					
520					X	O	X	O					
510					X	O	X	O					
500					X	O	X	O					
490					X	O							
480			X		X								
470			X	O	X								
460			X	O	X								
450	X		X	O									
440	X	O	X										
430	X	O	X										
420	X	O											
410	X												
400													

figure 6.18

another two Os in the same column at the price levels of 490p and 480p (Figure 6.19).

▨ The price reverses (y) and climbs to 503p. To establish a reversal and change columns you are looking for a price of not less than 510p. This price level does not meet the level required.

▨ The price drops again (z) to 419p. This amounts to a fall of 61p from the last full box plotted at 480p Put six Os in the same column at the price levels 470p, 460p, 450p, 440p, 430p and 420p (Figure 6.20).

▨ The price turns upwards (α) and reaches a level of 442p. You are looking for either a further drop to a level of 410p or lower, or a rise to a level of not less than 450p. This move does not fit either requirement. *Do nothing.*

▨ The price turns downwards again (β) and reaches a level of 417p. You require a fall of not less than 10p from the last full box plotted at 420p, which is 410p or lower. Not enough. *Do nothing.*

▨ The price turns upwards again (γ) and reaches a level of 476p, which is a reversal of 56p from the last O plotted at 420p. Start plotting Xs

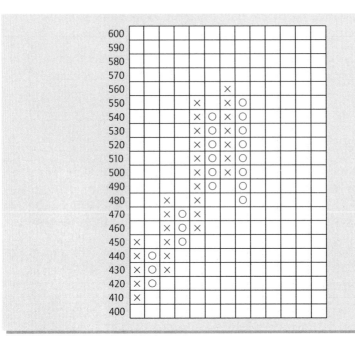

figure 6.19

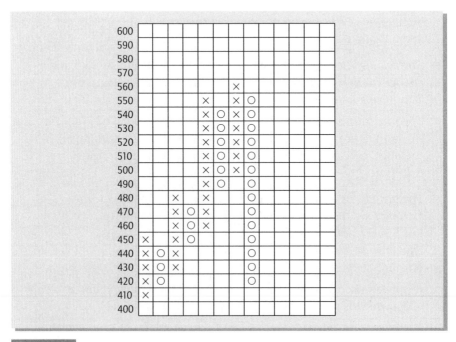

figure 6.20

in the next vertical column at the price levels 430p, 440p, 450p, 460p, and 470p (Figure 6.21).

■ The price continues upwards (δ) to 493p. This is 23p higher than the last box filled at 470p, so you must add another two Xs in the same column at price levels 480p and 490p (Figure 6.22).

Signals

Point and figure charts give buy and sell signals as well as indicating resistance and support levels in the same way that linear charts do. The strength of these signals varies also, and trend lines will help you to estimate the price levels at which you can expect to see a reversal, or possible break out.

The important point to remember, though, is that there will be no indication of time when any such event is likely to occur.

A summary of the main signals is given in Figures 6.23–6.29. Note that in point and figure charting, trend lines are always shown at angles of 45 degrees.

600													
590													
580													
570													
560						×							
550				×		×	○						
540				×	○	×	○						
530				×	○	×	○						
520				×	○	×	○						
510				×	○	×	○						
500				×	○	×	○						
490				×	○		○						
480			×		×		○						
470			×	○	×			○	×				
460			×	○	×			○	×				
450	×		×	○				○	×				
440	×	○	×					○	×				
430	×	○	×					○	×				
420	×	○						○					
410	×												
400													

figure 6.21

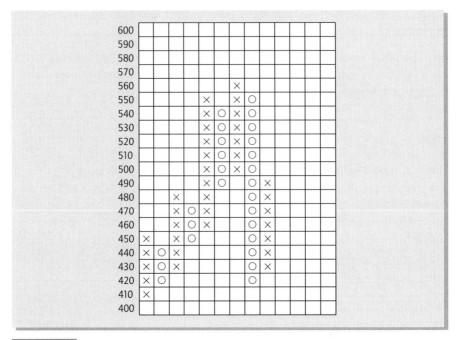

figure 6.22

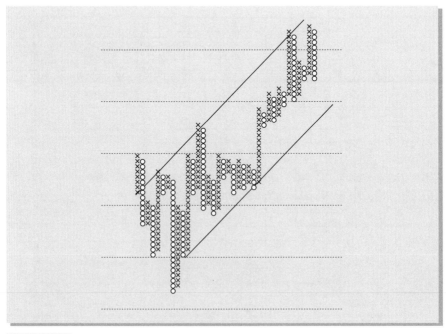

figure 6.23 Trading range uptrend (note trend lines always at 45 degrees)

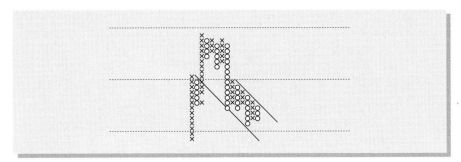

figure 6.24 Trading range in a downturn

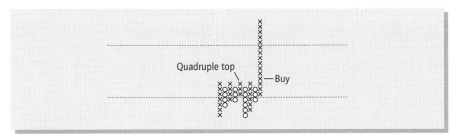

figure 6.25 Breakout upwards through a resistance level after a quadruple top

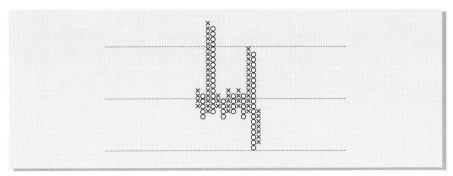

figure 6.26 Breakout both upwards and downwards

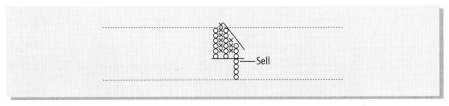

figure 6.27 Breakout downwards through a resistance level

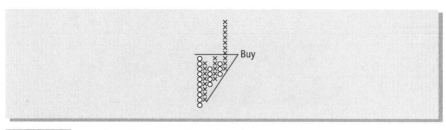

figure 6.28   Breakout from ascending triangle

The common feature to both ascending and descending triangles is a horizontal line, and the breakout always occurs going through that level. However, often you will see a breakout that is about to happen when neither line is horizontal, and they are converging towards a point like a horizontal > (Figure 6.29). When this happens, you have no way of knowing in which direction the breakout is likely to go, but it is a very strong signal. You have to watch it closely and make an investment quickly when you can see the direction appearing. A good example of three such occasions, showing two downwards and one upwards, is in Figure 6.29 from the historical price record of British Airways.

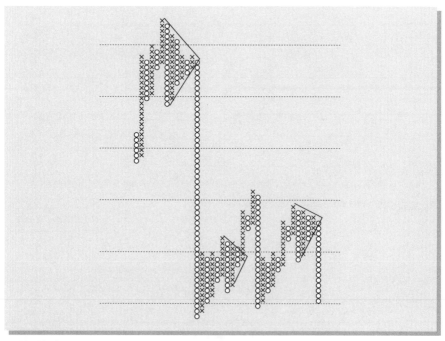

figure 6.29   Convergence towards a point – a very strong signal

Summary

In this chapter we have seen:

■ The way in which a point and figure chart is constructed.

■ Comparison with a linear chart.

■ Why point and figure charts give you a clearer picture.

■ The superior strength of signal of imminent price breakout compared with linear charts.

■ The inherent weakness in the inability to measure performance time, both past and future.

7

Building your portfolio

In this chapter we construct a strategy for investing for
recovery by:

- Setting performance targets.

- Asset allocation using property, bonds, commodities and
  equities.

- Using speculative investing, including short selling, until the
  market has established a recovery generally.

- Understanding adverse pressures that will affect the
  recovery.

Strategic planning

It is important that you establish your objectives and quantify your
targets. Ensure that each one is realistic and achievable in your timetable.
This exercise is your strategic planning.

The first action you must take sounds easy, but if you do it properly, it will
take longer than you think.

Set performance targets

■ Set targets for capital growth within short, medium and long-term objectives. Decide what you want to achieve when you have reached a certain date, such as retirement, children's university, marriage and death, and how much capital you think will be required to meet these objectives.

■ Calculate how much capital you have now that is available for investment. Estimate the annual percentage growth necessary on your capital to achieve your targets. Check your required growth rate with the average growth rate of the FTSE 250 share index and see whether your aspirations are reasonable and achievable, or whether you have to modify your targets. The historic growth rate claimed by market commentators in most cases does not include any erosion in the real value of money because of inflation, so remember it will be overstated in real terms. This is true whether you are considering sterling, dollars, euros, or any other currency. (Also, remember that examples of historical growth given by the managers of unit trusts, investment trusts, and other managed funds normally *exclude* the dealing costs of switching investments, and they assume that all income in 'growth' funds is reinvested net of basic rate tax only.) If you are a higher rate taxpayer, and had matched their investments exactly, you would not have achieved the same results as they claim.

■ Calculate how much income you will need for your retirement. Whilst this figure will vary massively for each person, for all the obvious reasons including age, employment terms and conditions, current pension provisions and so on, it is worth remembering that, as a rule of thumb in 2010, the sum of £500,000 (half a million pounds) is required to buy an annuity that will provide an annual *gross* income of £25,000. That is before tax. Any significant increase in inflation will diminish the real value of this income.

I strongly recommend that you keep a copy of all your detailed calculations, and note the reasons why you arrived at these figures, because memory is notoriously fallible. Also, since nothing ever goes exactly according to plan, it will help you very much when you come to modify and change your objectives as time passes and when unexpected events occur.

Above all, it will show you whether your demands of performance by your portfolio are reasonable and achievable, or not.

Only when you have established your performance criteria year by year for your target period should you move to the next step in your strategic planning.

Asset allocation

Why consider asset allocation in the first place? The reason is that it is a good idea to spread your risk. Clearly there is more risk attached to equities compared with fixed interest stock, such as gilts (or bonds) and they are both more risky than cash. Also, it is generally believed that one sector of investment will outperform the others over a given period, say a year, and is unlikely to continue to repeat the performance so you can switch your 'weighting' to another one that has performed poorly because there will be more room to make up with the obvious benefits attached. There is a school of thought that promotes a belief that it is worth buying shares at the beginning of a year in sectors that have underperformed during the previous year, because there will be shareholder pressure on the managements to pull their socks up and 'do much better next time'! When their share prices have recovered you should sell them and buy the next lot of 'underperformers'. That really is a lottery.

Nevertheless, it makes sense to spread your risk and so, on that score alone, it is a good idea to allocate your investment capital to different asset groups. I say investment capital as opposed to trading capital, which is dealt with separately.

I prefer to treat the question of asset allocation more as a safety factor concerned primarily with risk control and very much dictated by your own needs rather than as a formula for increasing profits or earnings. For example, anyone approaching retirement would rather increase their income and reinforce the safety of their capital than look for long-term growth, so that would influence their asset allocation choices in a different way from those in other circumstances. Unless, of course, if you have a good pension already arranged, then you may be prepared to speculate more with a view to increasing your capital base.

It is generally accepted that there are four main categories of asset in which to allocate your capital resources to provide growth or income. Your choice as to how much of your precious capital should be allocated to any, or all, will depend entirely on your individual circumstances and age and requirements.

Within each category there are investments that are more risky than others, and the question of risk evaluation will be dealt with in the next chapter. Here we are concerned only about the characteristics of each category, and what you can reasonably expect to get from each one. They are property, bonds, commodities and equities.

Property

The property market for investment consists of two categories, but there is one essential ingredient running through all of them. For long-term growth, as well as for optimum rental receipts, the most important factor is location. Anywhere that is considered a prime site, for whatever reason, will always be worth more and produce more capital growth and higher rents than those that are not thought to be so well situated.

However, there is a caveat. Investments in property, whether directly by your-self or using a managed fund that restricts its portfolio to properties, such as those operated by the larger insurance companies, can take much longer to liquidate than shares, which can be sold in a market at any time. Under normal market conditions this problem would not happen because the funds keep a cash balance aside to cope with expected liquidation requests. The crash of 2008 has shown how heavy and unexpected cash demands can occur, and the restrictions these can impose on the availability of liquid assets.

Recently, two property fund managers imposed a ban on liquidating investments in their funds, one for twelve months, and the other for six months, because the crash persuaded many investors to liquidate their portfolios and the funds ran out of cash reserves that are held specifically for paying out to sellers. The managers would have been forced to sell underlying properties at very substantial discounts to their values which would have been disastrous for the funds as well as penalising the other investors who wished to remain holders of their investments. Such actions, whilst very rare under normal circumstances, tend to cause panic among the non-professional investors and can often cause a run on the fund with corresponding adverse publicity which adds fuel to the fire. A good example of this can be seen in the behaviour of account holders in Northern Rock, which had to be nationalised to enable it to survive.

In the long term (twenty years or more), depending upon when you buy houses or flats in the cyclical housing market, I believe domestic property is probably the safest investment. The reason is simple. In Britain, the population is dense and increasing annually compared with the land mass, and land availability is finite. Governments can print as much money as they like (and devalue the currency in the process) but they cannot fabricate more land.

So long as there are attractive reasons for people to want to live and work in the UK, domestic property will remain in relatively short supply. It is this basic imbalance between supply and demand that will produce a good and steady return on your capital employed.

The greatest demand for city-centre living accommodation usually lies in the small one or two-bedroom flats, particularly those that are located close to railway stations or which have short travel times to commercial centres because these will always be easier to let. Historically these have shown the largest percentage increase in value over twenty years. However, the key to investment in this market is the cost of acquisition of the property in the first place. If you start from the general assumption that the gross annual rental income for a single bedroom purpose built flat in a city centre is probably around £1,000 a month, you can estimate the yield on any capital sum required to purchase the property easily. You must not forget to include agent's costs, and repairs and dilapidations in your expense calculations, as well as the annual cost of the capital if it has to be borrowed.

The UK commercial property market, including office, retail and factory buildings has fallen in value since 2008 by an average of 20 per cent, and is likely to continue to lose value, but not at such a fast rate. Estimates vary considerably, depending on where such properties are located, but – in late 2009 – generally it seems that a further drop of about 10 per cent is expected before prices stabilise.

Returns on investments made into this market were running at an exceptional average of 18 per cent in 2004–06, but they have now fallen to around 7 per cent per annum which is probably much more realistic, as well as being easier to maintain when the economy starts to gain more confidence.

Generally, you should not commit more than 10 per cent of your long-term investment capital into property. You must remember that although property share prices are much less likely to fluctuate and they are easily traded, the same considerations concerning the locations of their offices or shops or factories are of paramount importance in assessing the level of rental revenues they can command, and the financial standing of the tenants they can attract. British Land and Land Securities are the leading and largest property companies in the UK and their managements have built up many years of experience in these markets. They should be your benchmarks against which to judge others.

It is worth attending a specialised course to learn about returns on investment, gearing, loans to value, and getting independent expert advice on the subject before you commit yourself.

Bonds

Bonds are issued by a corporate borrower or a government that exchange them for money they wish to borrow over an extended and predetermined period and for which they are prepared to pay a fixed annual rate of interest for the duration of the period. They are redeemed by repayment of the nominal amount of each bond at the expiration of the period.

They are traded between investors in the same way that ordinary shares are bought and sold, and the price at which they are exchanged varies according to supply and demand, like any other financial instrument. Whilst the price may vary, the amount of interest they produce remains fixed and they are often called fixed-interest stocks. Generally, a bond has a life of not less than ten years at the time of issue.

The yield will rise or fall depending on the price level at which they are purchased.

The amount of interest that a company or government has to promise to pay on any bond issue depends on:

■ The credit rating (or perceived financial strength) of the issuer.
■ The cost of money, both actual currently and likely over the life of the proposed loan.

In the case of the UK government, until recently the safety of both interest and ultimate repayment has been considered to be impeccable, hence the label 'gilt-edged', or gilts.

However, on 25 March 2009, the Bank of England attracted just £1.67bn in bids for its sale of £1.75bn of 2049 gilts. It was the first time since 1995 that an auction of gilts was not covered fully. The market only bid for 93 per cent of the amount on offer (said to be 0.93 times covered), compared with the average cover of 2.1 times in the previous three auctions.

This failure raises fears that the government may not be able to secure the billions of pounds it needs from the markets to fund its record fiscal deficit without paying far more for the money, and reflects concerns about UK economic stability, which is a blow to the reputation of the financial management of the country.

In spite of this, the rate of interest attached to ten-year gilts (known as the 'coupon') is still used as the benchmark against which to measure all other rates of interest attached to corporate loans.

It is still assumed that the government will not default on either the payment of interest or capital and therefore represents the minimum risk in the market for loan stock.

Those shares that represent the largest companies measured by market capitalisation, i.e. the constituents of the FTSE 100, will normally be able to offer a rate of interest attached to any loan stock they may seek to issue just above that of gilts, and smaller companies perceived to be more risky still will have to offer even higher rates to attract investors.

As a general rule, the higher the rate of interest on offer, the higher the risk.

Obviously, since the market will dictate the price of all loan stocks during their lifetime, the *yield* will vary as the price moves up and down. As I have shown earlier, the lower the price, the more sellers there are than buyers. The sellers don't want the stock because they are unsure of its safety. The lower the price, the higher the yield.

Any stock that is offering returns that are too good to be true, probably is just that.

Bonds, or loans, come in various forms. Some are convertible into equities at some dates in the future at various formulae for calculating the conversion terms. Others, such as war loan, have no date for redemption and move up and down in price strictly in accordance with the level of interest rates.

Generally bonds are bought for safety of capital and reliable income purposes.

Index-linked gilts will become very attractive. The reasons are obvious. The vast amounts of money that have had to be pumped into the economy to support the failing banks and to try to kick-start commercial activities will exert strong inflationary pressures when the recovery starts again. So will rising oil prices and increasing wage demands. You should put at least a fifth of your capital to be invested for the longer term into these instruments.

Commodities

Commodities are probably the most dangerous investment that any non-professional investor can make. They are a recipe for disaster. They are very highly geared and it is imperative that anyone who is tempted to deal as a principal, buying or selling contracts in commodities, learns the business well before committing themselves, and also understands the risks and pitfalls in this volatile market. You really are well advised to use the services of an experienced fund manager whose fund has a good and proven track record, rather than doing it yourself.

Essentially, investing in commodities is just like investing in any other instrument, except that unless you actually wish to take delivery of the commodity and use it in your manufacturing process (such as a goldsmith, or a toolmaker, for example), you generally trade in future prices, and you buy if you think that the price is going to rise, and you sell short if you think the price is going to fall.

The trade is carried out in contracts, which can be for several tonnes of the commodity, but you deal on, say, a margin of 10 per cent, although your liability is for all of the price.

A good example of some of the problems facing the potential investor is the cocoa market. These are the brief facts concerning that product, and to be a successful investor you would have to be well informed about the main elements that can influence the price. Cocoa needs a hot, wet climate in which to grow. The main areas of production are East Africa, Indonesia and Brazil (55 per cent comes from the Cote d'Ivoire and Ghana, and 5 per cent from Nigeria). These countries are politically unstable and there are constant strikes. They regularly suffer from political and social upheavals which often affect production. There are no shortages of well publicised threats of strikes, often groundless, which can put immediate pressure on the price. Cocoa is also susceptible to 'black pod' disease, and even a rumour of an outbreak can affect prices.

Contracts are for ten tonnes (equivalent to 22,046 lb). The contract periods are March, May, July, September and December.

Cocoa is traded in dollars and the quotes are in dollars per ounce. Prices have ranged between $1,000 and $2,800 and hit a high of over $5,000 in 1977.

The last trading day to close a position in a futures contract is eleven business days before the last business day of the delivery month. You could end up with a truck containing 10 tonnes of cocoa beans at your door with the driver asking where you would like him to unload it!

As with most investments, experience bred from long association with the trade and the companies that are active within it enables those individuals to know where the pitfalls lie, what rumours to discount and which ones matter. You are best advised to take the advice of someone who is experienced in the vicissitudes of the commodity markets and able to act on your behalf, or guide you through the minefield. There are good profits to be made, but most of us need expert help, if for no other reason than to limit the downside risks which are ever present.

Commodities that are traded are:

Corn	Cocoa	Ethanol	Silver
Oats	Coffee	Natural gas	Copper
Rice	Cotton	Heating oil	Lead
Soybeans	Sugar	Propane	Zinc
Rapeseed	Hogs	Gold	Tin
Soybean meal	Pork bellies	Uranium	Aluminium
Soybean oil	Cattle	Platinum	Nickel
Wheat	Oil	Palladium	

The main exchanges are:

Chicago Mercantile Exchange; Commodity Futures Trading Commission; London International Financial Futures and Options Exchange; National Futures Association; New York Mercantile Exchange; Kansas City Board of Trade; and New York Board of Trade

Probably the safest way to trade commodities is by using exchange traded funds (ETF) but using the expertise of a fund manager or adviser, and paying their charges. Commodities can be used to form part of a portfolio and make substantial contributions to the portfolio value over a short period, but to limit your risk as much as possible, you need to have an ability to watch the prices all the time during market hours and often this is not possible for people who have other commitments in their daily lives.

Equities

Traditionally, equities have been considered to be the mainframe of the machine you need to construct to build up your capital over a period. This may be relatively short term, say a few years with a specific objective in mind such as paying for children's university fees, weddings, or a specific event that you consider more or less inevitable. Or it could be to provide a pension or additional income on retirement.

Whatever the objective, the equity market usually bears the brunt of the burden to perform and increase the wealth of the investor as well as to provide additional income from dividends. It is this last point that you should remember as being the foundation stone on which you should base all your financial planning.

Simply remember that the fundamental reason why individuals and pension fund managers buy shares is for income:

- *Increased income, whether actual or anticipated, creates demand for individual shares.*
- *Increased demand pushes up the price. A higher price means capital gain.*

To find individual shares that will outperform the market *and* to reduce the risk of loss to the minimum is what this book is all about. I shall now describe the disciplines and show you how to find these opportunities.

Tactical planning

So, how can you achieve the objectives and targets set out in your strategic planning? The quest for opportunities to increase your wealth and income will inevitably be shaped and influenced by the stock market. The US investor Warren Buffett has claimed that it is impossible to forecast with any accuracy where the market will be more than a few months ahead because of unexpected occurrences. Harold Macmillan, when he was prime minister, claimed that nothing ever went according to plan because of 'events'.

Some economists are currently predicting economic Armageddon, including a long period of deflation similar to that which has plagued Japan for ten years. Others differ in their opinions as to the shape of the recession as well as their estimates as to how long it will be before any recovery begins. Some believe that the bottom of the market has been reached and passed already, whilst others think that what we are experiencing is what is known in the market as a 'dead cat' bounce. This occurs when a market falls rapidly, reaches a low, then it recovers several points and continues its downward movement. It is important not to get sucked into believing the hype and false confidence that is generated inevitably by those investors and newspaper scribes who enthuse about the market turnround because that is what they want to believe.

Very often such false dawns are created by bear closing activity. This occurs when investors who have taken out short positions are forced to buy the shares, albeit at a considerable loss to themselves, to close their positions. It is frequently exacerbated also by those who really do think that the market has turned and are buying in order to get in at the lowest price possible.

▦ Golden rule: After a sustained fall, *always* wait to see a trend established for any share price before you buy.

Stock market prices always represent investors' opinion of the earnings position of each stock and share *six months ahead*. These opinions are based on fundamentals rather than political or world economic factors. If, for example, it was widely expected that the price of oil would rise by a significant amount in the next six months, then the share prices of those companies that provide transport services as their main activity would be most affected. Obviously, the cost of moving goods would be increased, but other companies might be able to absorb these extra costs without having to increase their selling prices to the consumer. For example, it would increase the delivery costs of all foodstuffs supplied by the supermarkets and other retail outlets, but their share prices would not be expected to react as much.

▦ Golden rule: Think laterally. If you see or hear an adverse comment or proposal (e.g. imminent taxation increase, or government directive) that might have a bearing on a company's profitability, check immediately with the other similar companies in the same sector to see whether you can get a short-term profit by selling their shares short. *Only compare like with like.*

The corollary is equally true. If there has been good news about a product, it may well benefit the company's share price, and you should see whether there could be a knock-on effect with the prices of other similar companies.

There are more than 3,000 companies listed on the London Stock Exchange and it is impossible to get to know each one intimately. But you really do need to know as much as you can about the companies in which you are investing your precious capital long term, or trading some of it short term. No one can be an expert in all of them. It will pay you handsomely to specialise and concentrate your research in two, or at most three sectors, and build up in-depth knowledge about the companies within these areas of commerce. As you would expect, each sector will include large, medium and small companies (measured by market capitalisation) and often the extent and scope of their activities will vary, sometimes greatly.

For example, in the Oil & Gas sector in the *Financial Times*, there are the leaders in the industry, many of which are household names, together with smaller companies that specialise in aspects of the discovery, extraction, refining, distribution and retailing of the substance. Each of them has different needs and requirements, as well as different reactions to changes in global circumstances such as the price of crude, currency exchange rates, central bank interest rates and political or regime changes. Some, such as Royal Dutch Shell, BP, Exxon Mobil, Total and OGX undertake all the processes from prospecting through refining and distribution to retailing the final products as well as marketing the byproducts from the refining process, such as ethanol, benzine and tar. They are very large companies and their power is enormous, particularly in underdeveloped countries. Their annual expenditure in prospecting alone is often greater than the whole economy of several small countries. Their financial resources are massive, but so are their capital requirements.

Then there are smaller companies such as Cairn Energy, Tullow, Emerald and others, which specialise in prospecting for oil and gas fields. When they find one, they hawk it round the big boys to get the highest price per barrel as a royalty on all oil extracted by the company to whom they sell the franchise. Their capital requirements are very small compared with the majors because they have no involvement with the extraction, refining and distribution of the crude. They prosper when interest rates are low and the price of crude is high. If interest rates climb to near 10 per cent a year, many of the smaller prospecting-only companies stop their activities and wait until the economics are more favourable. Sometimes these companies will earn further income by waiting for the contract to revert to them when the major has extracted 70–80 per cent of the original reserves and find that the cost of extracting the remainder is uneconomic. At that point, the company negotiates another contract with another smaller oil company that can afford to work the residue because it has not had the expense of developing the field and can take over the existing infrastructure without any capital expenditure. Finally, there are small distribution companies, such as Dragon Oil, that specialise in providing bulk storage (e.g. jet fuel storage for aircraft at remote aerodromes in China) and retail sales stations. Profit margins are usually low, and their markets are small. Interest rates and exchange rates have a disproportionate effect on their success. They can be vulnerable to political changes.

You can see why it is so important to understand fully the companies that you select for investment, because then your judgement will be much more acute and you will be able to make much better decisions as to what to buy and when to buy and sell.

■ Golden rule: Remember that successful investing is as much about controlling risk as it is about finding and picking winners.

The shape of the recession

If one knew how long the recession was likely to last, one could be sure of making profits. My crystal ball does not have the necessary add-ons to give me this vital piece of news, but at least I am not alone in this state of ignorance. I do not believe anyone else has one that can tell them the answer either, but the facts that are known offer a good pointer as to the probable pattern that will emerge, and experience will be a reliable guide to the investment practices that will enable one to build in safety factors such as risk controls, as well a much better than average chance of making good profits. Before I explain how to achieve these results, let us look at the facts as they are at the end of 2009.

Government debt

The government debt has been allowed to mount up to levels never seen before in the history of Britain. The OECD has forecast that the deficit will climb to 90 per cent of economic output. Currently this debt is estimated at £2.2 trillion, a figure that has trebled since the government bailed out the banks in trouble. That figure considerably understates the problem because the enormous pensions' shortfall is not included. The governor of the Bank of England described the situation as a 'truly extraordinary' scale of deficits. The IMF has said that it thinks the situation will get worse and unemployment will rise. The Institute for Fiscal Studies has said that it will take twenty-three years to get government borrowing down to any reasonable levels.

Why does all this matter to investors?

Rising unemployment produces two economic disasters. First, the tax revenues are reduced because the unemployed are not receiving any taxable income and, second, the cost to the taxpayer of paying benefits to the unemployed increases. The only source of income available to the government is taxation, both individual and corporate, so the government increases the deficit by borrowing to cover the shortfall.

The higher the deficit, the more likely it becomes that the international credit rating agencies, such as Standard & Poor's, will downgrade the highest level of triple A that is enjoyed by Britain, and has been since the rating system was started, so that it will make government borrowing from international lenders more expensive, as well as reducing the value of sterling in relation to other currencies. Overseas investors are more likely to liquidate their investments in Britain and move their activities abroad, which in turn will increase the levels of unemployment and reduce profits in the UK.

The main reasons for investing in any situation are safety of capital and attractive earnings, with the likelihood of earnings growth each year. This applies as much to the private individual investor as it does to companies and institutional or government bodies.

The shape of the recession has been the subject of many speculative articles in the press and on television.

Some have said that it will be V-shaped. That is to say that the market will drop to a certain level and then change direction and climb back to continued growth and rising share prices. There is absolutely no evidence to support this view, particularly when you consider the facts described above.

Some subscribe to the theory that it will be W-shaped. They point to the mini-recovery in May/June 2009 as supporting their theory, and there has been a lot of coverage given to anyone who can be found to express the view that 'the green shoots of recovery' are discernable among the corporate results recently announced. I do not agree with this view either. Order books are not demonstrating any increase in future industrial activity, and unemployment is continuing to rise, as is the number of house repossessions.

I believe that the shape of the recession is much more likely to be that of an elongated L with the greatest unknown being the length of the horizontal leg. Demand for investment in equities will wait until a clear picture emerges with detailed plans showing how the government intends to deal with the debt mountain, and the changes these will bring to the levels of corporate taxation, costs of borrowing, and the estimated effects on future earnings that will follow.

Three further items that will exert continuing and long-term adverse pressures on earnings will be corporate taxation, inflation and oil prices. You must always be prepared to change any long-term investment if it seems that their future anticipated earnings or growth may be hit by substantial rises in costs resulting from increases in any of these corrosive elements.

However, there are two elements which will undoubtedly occur:

■ There will continue to be considerable volatility in the stock market.

■ There will be plenty of opportunities to make money by trading in these volatile markets.

I shall divide the type of market exploitation into two parts. Speculative short-term trading, and longer-term hold, i.e. a portfolio.

Summary

In this chapter we have explained why you need to:

■ carefully construct performance targets that are realistic and achievable;

■ allocate your assets, noting why you have made your selections and reviewing them every year;

■ use short-term trading initially to augment capital growth arising from your long-term portfolio selection.

8

How to find winners while limiting risk

In this chapter we show how to apply the disciplines imposed by fundamental analysis together with the signals that are thrown up using technical analysis to:

■ Find suitable candidates for short and long-term investments.

■ Trade indices.

■ Trade equities.

■ Control your risks.

Speculative short-term trading

What do I mean by speculative short-term trading? It is the tactic of finding an instrument which is undervalued, or where the price follows a pattern of movement up and down that is eminently predictable within a trading range, and investing in it for a few days or weeks to make a profit *and then converting the paper gain into cash*.

These opportunities are easier to find in a downtrend within a falling market, and the potential for profit is greater and faster when investing in a price fall than it is in a price rise. 'Investing' means using CFDs or financial spread betting to sell short. It means using CFDs or financial spread betting to exploit a rising price. When you use CFDs, your transaction is based on the cash price of a stock or share with the advantage of close spreads. Financial spread betting is based on the futures prices, not the cash prices.

Trading an index

The best example to use for this type of exploiting a volatile market is to use financial spread betting and bet on an index, such as the Dow Jones Industrial Average index (the Dow Jones) or the FTSE 100.

Whatever instrument you choose to bet on, whether it is a company share price, or an index, *you must impose a stop-loss limit when you place the bet*. This is essential so that you know exactly what your potential loss might be, and you should write off the amount of the potential loss when you place the bet. This will ensure that you have calculated what the loss might be and you know that you can afford it, should things not go as you anticipate.

Financial spread bet prices are based on the futures prices, not the spot market prices, and they don't always move exactly in tandem. However, to illustrate the technique, I have used spot market prices in the examples shown.

The first step when looking at any short-term trading opportunity is to establish the trend. You must know whether the price is trending up, down or sideways.

Figure 8.1 shows the historical record of the Dow Jones using daily closing prices since October 2007. Throughout 2007 and 2008 the trend was downwards. Then came the October 2008 crash.

The line chart is still trending downwards, with an established trading range between about 8,300 and 8,800. If the point and figure chart establishes a downwards box *below* the level of the last four downward movements shown in Figure 8.2 with a resistance line drawn under them (say 50 points below 8,300), then you should place a down bet on the index. Figure 8.2 shows the point and figure chart for the period mid January 2009 to the end of June 2009. This chart is based on box size of 50 points using a three-box reversal.

It may be a useful exercise to restrict your betting *when a new direction has been established* so that you *only* place a bet to open *after* four boxes have become established in the new column. Also, restrict your betting to the direction of the trend. If the trend overall is downwards, you will reduce

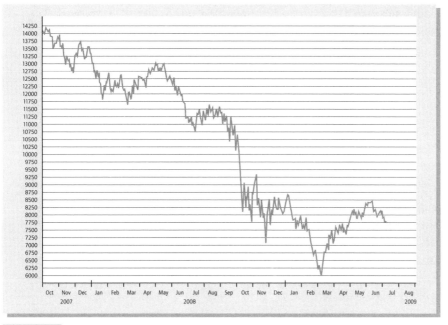

figure 8.1   Dow Jones Industrial index (October 2007–July 2009)   Source: Updata plc

your risk of loss if you only place down bets until the trend has demonstrated that it has really established a change of direction.

Place a trailing stop-loss limit of 50 points (in this case) when you open the bet.

When you open a position using an index such as the FTSE 100 or the Dow Jones in the current volatile market conditions, if there is a trend established in one direction, it will also be prudent to place any bets to open when the point and figure chart indicates a change in direction (e.g. from 'down' to 'up') only when there have been five boxes established, still using the trailing one-box stop-loss.

You can see from Figure 8.1 how this would have turned out. By mid July 2009 the Dow had dropped to 8,150 from about 14,000 in October 2008.

Golden rule

Whether you are looking at an index or a share price to trade short term, *do not be in a hurry to open any bets*. You will cut down greatly the chances of making losses, and it is better to win a smaller amount rather than lose anything.

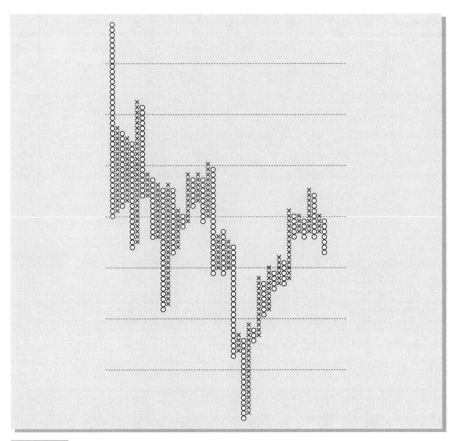

figure 8.2 Dow Jones point and figure chart (three-box reversal; 50 points box size) from mid January 2009 to end of June 2009

Trading a share

The same procedures apply to establishing the trend of a share and establishing the trading range so that you can see how far the latest movement is likely to go before you would expect it to change direction. You can also evaluate the price at which you expect this change to take place so that you are able to judge whether there is sufficient profit potential to warrant an investment at this point, or whether it would be better to wait for the change to occur and then take a position. This cautionary discipline is illustrated by the pattern shown by Tate & Lyle shares shown in Figure 8.3.

It would be best to use contracts for difference (CFDs) for this short-term equity trading because the gearing (or leverage) is working to your advantage.

Source: Updata plc

figure 8.3 Tate & Lyle share price

You should start by looking for a share where there is plenty of movement in the price, and one that has a substantial volume of trades every day. Penny shares, or companies with a market capitalisation of under £400m are not likely to meet the criteria you need, and the price spreads for such smaller companies will work against you.

Figure 8.4 shows the point and figure chart for Tate & Lyle for the period from December 2007 to 13 July 2009, using a box size of 20p with a three-box reversal. You can see the downward trend very much confirmed by this chart.

Figure 8.5 shows the trading range for the share price of Tate & Lyle superimposed on the line chart of the share price. At first sight it looks as if you can be reasonably certain of making money by investing in an upward movement in this share *only* when it has turned within the trading range limit. But the overall trend is downwards and I should not be tempted to adopt any risk on an upward bet until the long-term trend has shown a change in direction for several months. There are better opportunities.

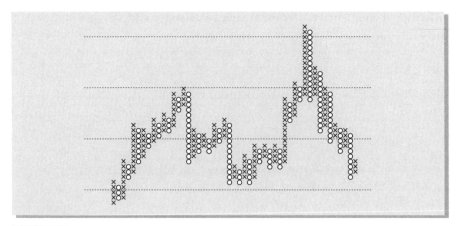

figure 8.4 Tate & Lyle point and figure chart

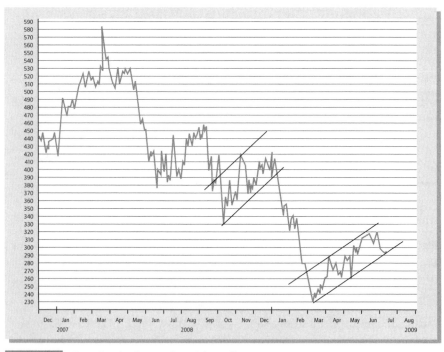

figure 8.5 Tate & Lyle share price with trading ranges

Source: Updata plc

If, for any reason, the price were to break through the trading range upwards, you should wait to see if this change becomes well established before putting any capital at risk.

You should *always* make a record of your calculations and your reasoning behind your investment decisions together with your anticipated target prices and direction change levels so that if the price behaves erratically, you can see whether it is necessary to cut your investment.

In all cases, if the price moves against your calculations, cut your loss.

Golden rule

The first cut is always the cheapest cut. *Never* hang on to a share whose price is moving against you in the hope that it will recover.

Short-term trading investments made in indices or equities or commodities should be monitored every day at the very least. Targets should be set and records kept for every investment made, together with the points that you established during your research before taking the investment decision.

You should be on the look-out all the time that you are exposed to risk for any news that might have an effect on your investments and act accordingly. For instance, there is no doubt that government expenditure is going to be cut to reduce the huge deficit in the economy. When any announcements are made, perhaps such as a cancellation of military hardware (ships, aircraft, weapons, etc.) consider whether any of the companies in which you have current investments might be affected by cancelled orders or loss of sub-contract work, and act accordingly.

You have to monitor short-term trading investments even more closely than you would for a long-term growth portfolio. It is hard work, but the rewards should fully justify your vigilance.

Building your portfolio for long-term growth

The steps to follow are:

▪ Find a share.

▪ Do your fundamental analytical homework.

▪ Set your targets and objectives.

▪ Monitor the progress of each one regularly.

▪ Keep a profit/loss account of each investment.

Find a share

There are so many 'tip sheets' nowadays that you are spoiled for choice. In fact you can't avoid being bombarded with articles and claims of phenomenal gains and continuous success rates that some 'guru' has achieved, most of them inviting you to subscribe to a service that will let you enjoy their supply of winners from now on.

You can get such a wide range of recommendations from journals such as the *Investors' Chronicle*, through numerous web pages on your PC, to the old original source – 'a chap in the pub'! The source doesn't matter; it's what you do with the tip that does.

There are several managers of quite large funds who spend at least a couple of hours a day, every day, looking through share price charts until they see a pattern that they recognise as useful. Of course, this ability comes from practice, but you can learn the rudiments of such signal recognition quite easily and it is a useful way to start. Certainly, you do not need to pay for such information.

I use, and highly recommend, a data source called ADVFN which has the great advantage of being free and it is very comprehensive in its coverage of all the information required. The website provides charts for individual share performance, and current and historical analysis as well. You will see examples of the extent and scope of information they provide in this section of the book since I have used their data to illustrate the points that I want to make. Simply type www.advfn.com and you can get all the information you need, free.

I have chosen two companies to illustrate points that I shall develop in the next step (fundamental and technical analytical homework), rather than because they would be my prime choices for profits. As I explained earlier, you need to compare like with like, and there are some very interesting lessons to be learned here. The companies are A.G. Barr and Britvic. Both manufacture and distribute soft drinks.

Fundamental and technical analytical homework

The main purpose of this analytical homework is twofold. First, it should give you a really good 'feel' for a company; its size, its financial strengths and weaknesses, its track record, and it should enable you to form an opinion about its management attitudes and competence. Second, it will raise questions for which you may need to get answers before you expose your capital to risk.

In this step we shall examine the important figures, financial ratios, operating ratios and profit and loss account fundamentals, among other aspects. Individual item results may contradict other figures, or confirm them. It is more important to look at the trends of each item where possible so that you get a good idea of where the company is going. You can also factor into the emerging picture any outside event that may be beyond the control of management, but you can see what effect such an event had on the company's performance and whether one company coped more or less efficiently with such a setback, or boost.

Do not be daunted by the extent and scope of the figures and ratios to be analysed; at first sight it looks like a lot of work. With practice you will find it easy to recognise whether figures are relatively good or bad, and the exercise, done frequently and as a matter of course, will hone your judgement skills. It is *your* money that is going to be put at risk, so you have a vested interest in checking for any pitfalls yourself.

You start by looking at linear charts to find share price patterns that demonstrate the following characteristics. Momentum (plenty of oscillation up and down over two or three years and currently). An obvious trend, whether upwards or downwards is immaterial, or showing several substantial changes in direction. A clear and wide trading range.

Then you look at the key figures and ratios obtained from analysis of the Profit and Loss Accounts and Balance Sheets over the last five years to confirm the financial health and management ability (or lack of either), and see whether there is a positive or negative trend emerging from these analyses.

This homework will let you build two lists of companies. One list of those that are potential candidates for capital growth investments, and these must show evidence of sustained increases in earnings over a five-year period, and the second list that are worth considering for short-term trading, either up or down. It doesn't matter whether your analysis shows the company's health to be good or bad, since you can make good profits from short selling a falling share price just as you can gain by buying a rising price. That is why you need a wide trading range and plenty of movement of the share price to see that there is enough potential gain to give you a profit after covering dealing costs.

Do NOT forget to limit your downside risk by always waiting to ensure the share price movement has confirmed its reversal of direction before you commit your capital and opened your exposure to risk.

The data required for analyses of the three companies chosen to illustrate this approach are shown in the Appendices. Appendix 1 covers A.G. Barr, Appendix 2 covers Britvic, and Appendix 3 covers Severn Trent.

Table 8.1 uses the explanations of the key figures and ratios to show comparisons of these analyses between A.G. Barr and Britvic – both companies in the soft drinks sector – to demonstrate the steps you should take to make a decision whether or not to invest, or simply watch their progress as potential future investment candidates. It always pays to keep copies of your homework and written reasons for your conclusions because it will save you a lot of time in the future if their circumstances change substantially.

Severn Trent provides an example of what to look for in a 'trading' share.

Appendix 1 gives part of the report and accounts for A.G. Barr and Appendix 2 shows the same for Britvic, as well as their summary data from ADVFN. These can be analysed to produce the summaries given in Table 8.1.

table 8.1 Summary data for A.G. Barr and Britvic

	A.G. Barr	Britvic
Share price (p)	1,240	280
Previous high (12 months)	1,370	311
Potential gain (p)	130	31
Potential gain (%)	10.4	11

There is not much potential upside in either case.

Clearly the product sales are going to be enhanced if there is a long, hot summer, and vice versa, but normally neither of these companies would look like attractive propositions on this data.

Market cap. (£m)	241.32	605.17

A.G. Barr is a small company at the lower end of the range. It makes and markets fewer products than Britvic, and its distribution is mainly in

Scotland and Northern England. Britvic has a bigger range of products to sell and covers the UK.

Earnings per share (p)	89.12	14.90

The large difference between the two companies is because A.G. Barr has a much greater proportion of equity to capital employed than Britvic, where the proportion of borrowings is much higher (see *gross gearing* and *pre-tax profit per share* below). Borrowings, whether secured or unsecured, are more expensive to service than equity (which is another form of borrowing but without the risk of recall by a lender) and they are especially risky in the current economic downturn. The cost of borrowing, either from banks or institutional sources will certainly go up when interest rates rise and inflation returns.

Dividend per share (p)	42	11

The discrepancy is caused by the different share capital structure as described under the item *EPS* above.

Dividend cover (times)	2.12	1.35

This is one of the most important figures that you need. It demonstrates the extent to which the directors are exercising good husbandry and keeping the distribution of profits to a reasonable proportion while putting aside in reserve an adequate amount of earnings. Any company that is showing a dividend cover figure of less than 1 should be avoided unless there is an exceptional reason for ignoring this caveat.

Dividend yield (%)	3.39	3.93

The best way to look at this number is to ask yourself the question 'If I had to borrow the money to buy this share, would the yield be more than enough to cover the cost?' Of course, you will be expecting some growth as well, and the yield is based on a historical dividend payment, but you must satisfy yourself that your capital is earning its keep, and if the yield is not high enough, what makes you think that the growth will more than compensate for the shortfall in income in real terms? Don't forget to allow for the erosion in values from annual inflation. A low yield coupled with low growth expectations should put you off the share.

PE ratio	13.91	18.79

The lower the PE ratio compared with others in the same sector, the more the share price is considered to be undervalued by the market.

PE to PE average (%)	96.71	110.78

The market is not anticipating much growth from either company. Furthermore, you should ask yourself whether the analysis of the Britvic figures justify the above average rating which suggests that there has been some general expectation of growth (and a corresponding increase in the share price) recently.

Return on capital employed (ROCE) (%)	15.68	10.91

This is probably the most important ratio of all, and you really need to see a trend by looking at the record over the last five years to get a good feel about the efficiency of the management. One year's result does not give you a true picture. It is the measure of how good, or otherwise, the management is at building up wealth for the shareholders, after all costs have been deducted. You are looking for a steadily rising trend line.

Of equal importance are the quick ratio and the current ratio, both shown below.

Quick ratio (acid test)	0.94	0.65

This ratio, often called the 'acid test', should not be lower than 1. Preferably 2 or 3. It denotes the company's ability to meet its day-to-day obligations. It includes cash plus accounts receivable and liquidatable investments

Current ratio	1.32	0.83

This ratio should be slightly higher than the quick ratio, and certainly greater than 1. It includes cash plus accounts receivable and stock, or inventory. The only worry would be the price at which stock, or inventory, could be converted into cash in a short time.

PEG factor	5.09	−0.7

A PEG ratio is an indicator of a possible true value of a share because it embodies an element of future growth, allowing for the values of costs commensurate with higher growth. However, this element is not based on any fact and assumes a factor of growth that may be unrealistic, so the signal that it gives should be regarded as a possible indication rather than having any real basis in fact. It is important that the figures used in the calculation for EPS are future estimates rather than historical ones.

As a rule of thumb, a PEG of 0 to 1 is considered to indicate more growth potential than a PEG with a higher figure.

Earnings per share (EPS) growth rate (%)	2.73	−26.96

Another figure that demonstrates the degree of efficiency of management to make the business increase wealth for its shareholders.

Gross gearing (%)	50.52	98.75

Gearing, or leveraging, can enhance shareholders' returns substantially, particularly if the cost of borrowed funds is well below the percentage of net profits that such additional production and sales generates. However, under the current economic conditions, substantial borrowing compared with the amount of equity in the company can put the company at the mercy of its creditors. Heavy gearing should make you wary of investing without reading the chairman's statement carefully. If the subject is not raised and discussed in the statement, you should be very cautious.

Net gearing (%)	46.85	96.83

The same comments apply to the net gearing ratios as they do to the gross gearing figures. In these cases, when you analyse the pre-tax profit per share for each company, the difference in management efficiency is even more clearly defined.

Net debt (£m)	87.57	717.8

A figure that is particularly important currently. When inflation returns, the cost of a high level of debt could become a problem unless it can be cut. Such reduction can really only be achieved by substituting debt for equity, for example by having a rights issue. However, remember that if you are a shareholder and are unable or unwilling to take up your rights, the percentage of your holding in the company will be diluted.

Net working capital (£m)	12.3	−44.3

Beware of any company whose figures show a negative value for this item. Positive net working capital means that the company is able to pay its short-term debts, such as creditors. A lack of working capital means the company does not have enough cash or short-term debtors or stock that is readily convertible into cash. This could lead to a cessation of trading, or even bankruptcy.

Net asset value per share (p)	476.15	4.3

A somewhat theoretical figure arrived at by dividing the current value of the net assets of a company by the number of shares in issue. This presupposes that the book values could be converted into cash if the assets were sold. Generally considered unlikely and overstated under forced sale conditions. However, it gives you a benchmark, although this figure will always be lower than the market price for the share.

There are many more analytical items available from the data in the Appendix, but the main ones that you need to record are listed above. It may seem at first to be daunting to carry out the analysis but without the data, you are operating blindfolded.

Having carried out the fundamental analysis, the next step is to do the technical analytical homework.

Consider the share price chart of each company:

- Start with Figure 8.6 (A.G. Barr) and Figure 8.7 (Britvic). Although the share prices of both companies plummeted in October 2008 along with the rest of the market, the price of A.G. Barr recovered substantially stronger (and with a much higher price per share) than did that of Britvic.

- Figures 8.6 and 8.7 show that both shares have established an upward trend since February 2009. The trading range of A.G. Barr shows a movement of about 100p fairly consistently, whereas there is no reliable pattern established for Britvic.

- The values between the support and resistance levels for Britvic (the potential for profit) are not large enough to be interesting, nor is there any substantial momentum. However, there is an interesting pattern for A.G. Barr. You can see that the share price has dropped from the end of September until mid-December for the past two years. The time to buy this share is *after the price has turned upwards* in January, and bank the profits *after the price has turned downwards* in January/February.

figure 8.6 The share price chart for A.G. Barr shows a trading range of about 100p and an interesting seasonal trading pattern   Source: Updata plc

figure 8.7 No reliable trend pattern can be established for Britvic and the support and resistance levels are not wide enough to be interesting Source: Updata plc

There are other shares that produce patterns of this type. You have to keep looking for them, and you will find them using linear charts.

■ Figures 8.8 and 8.9 show the point and figure charts for the two companies. Bearing in mind the pattern of A.G. Barr referred to above, I should expect to see the fall in October confirmed in the chart as well as the recovery in December. In this case I should wait for a four-box movement to be shown, in either direction, before investing, and then make a substantial commitment using CFDs with a two-box trailing stop-loss. You can see what kind of results that would have produced in the past, and how many times I would have not become exposed to risk. The chart of Britvic confirms my view that this company would not qualify for an investment in the current economic climate, and I am not impressed by its performance.

In the days before the advent of personal computers, only the professional fund management firms had access to this information, and the private client was excluded from all this knowledge, unless he or she took the trouble to work out all the ratios and percentages from the published report and accounts for each company.

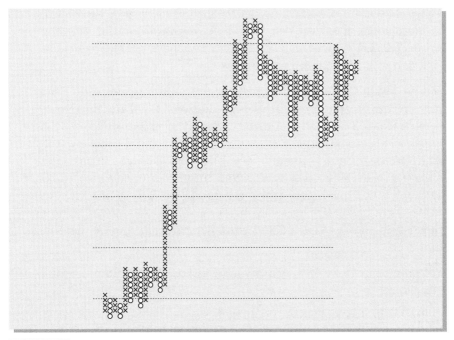

figure 8.8 Point and figure chart for A.G. Barr (three box and 15 points)

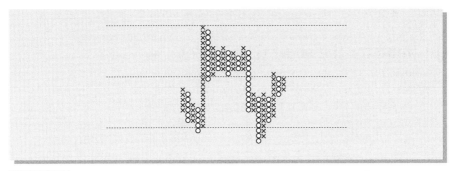

figure 8.9 Point and figure chart for Britvic (three box and 15 points)

Now such data is freely available, and the purpose of this book is to show you how to use it and benefit from the knowledge such analysis gives you to make your wealth grow.

The chief executive's statement for A.G. Barr is shown in Appendix 1.

I have chosen this pair of companies for analysis to illustrate two points. In my opinion, it is clear that, from a management point of view, the smaller company is better run and I believe that any capital investment in A.G. Barr would be exposed to a lower risk.

Second, I want to stress the fact that your attitude to stock selection must be 'very hard to please'. It is essential that you do all the homework before making a decision, but even so, do not be in a hurry to commit any precious capital until you really get excited about a company. Too many private investors want to be persuaded that they have either found a winner, or feel that they can't afford to miss an opportunity when someone with a glib tongue makes them feel privileged to be invited to 'make a killing' by buying some shares. As I have said earlier, 'Where there's a tip, there's a tap' and the person whispering in your ear wants to turn it on.

You must expect to reject very many more investment opportunities than you accept.

Control your risks and be very choosey. Remember that until market conditions return to normal, when the uncertainty of political influences have been substantially resolved and bank relationships with their customers return to normal, you cannot build long-term portfolios with any certainty. You must use short-term trading to build capital and take profits quickly and frequently. There will be plenty of such opportunities[1].

Severn Trent: for the short-term trader

Now let us look at the sort of company whose product and share price pattern have much appeal and should be interesting to any short-term trader. The company is one of the constituents of the FTSE 100. It is called Severn Trent and it is in the business of supplying water and sewage services – both which are vital for everyone. It also has a near monopoly in its area. Appendix 3 shows the ADVFN data for the company.

---

1 Subsequently, in October 2009, A.G. Barr subdivided the denomination of the 25p ordinary shares, and issued two 12.5p ordinary shares instead for every 25p share, so the holders of the 25p shares then held double the number. The market price of each 25p share was about 1,260p, so the new 12.5p shares would have been about 630p. By the end of December the price had climbed to around 905p, equivalent to about 1,810 per old 25p share.

This share is a trader's delight, as can be seen from Figure 8.10. Just look at the volatility of the share price and the frequency with which it rises and falls. This is called momentum, and the more there is, the more money you can make.

Although the company is big, with a market capitalisation of £2,612m, you should still carry out the fundamental analytical homework to satisfy yourself that it is not about to go belly up. This can happen to any company, however big or small, and you should get into the habit of doing your research as a matter of course anyway.

Since we are looking at this company with a view to exposing capital to short-term risk (say from two to four months) and we are not concerned with deriving an income from any long-term investment, the most important controls are the quick ratio, which is 1.43, and the current ratio, which is 1.47. So the company can meet its current liabilities. The EPS is negative, and although the company has reported a drop in profits for the year ending 31 March 2009, down from £192m to £168m, it increased its dividend pay-out to 67.34p a share whilst bad debts grew by £6.8m to £38m. The company blamed lower commercial usage. It is seeking approval from the industry regulator to increase its prices.

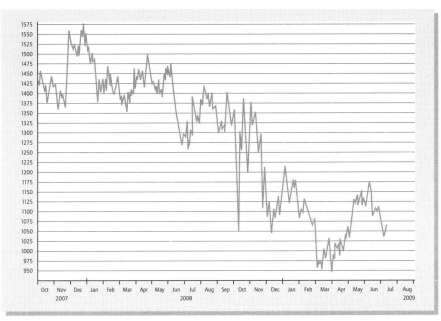

figure 8.10 Share price chart for Severn Trent – note the level of volatility, which offers the potential for profit

Source: Updata plc

From a long-term investing point of view, I would not recommend putting capital at risk where the management increases dividends when making losses. Although the situation in this type of near monopolistic undertaking is different from the normal commercial business that has to compete with other companies in the same market for its products or services, there is no need to increase the risks to your investment by taking a long position in any company where either the turnover or profits are declining. It is better to wait until they have changed direction and become positive.

The company has said that it plans to invest £20 million, compared with its previous expectation of about £12 million, to deliver an additional £5 million of cost savings in 2009 to 2010. It is not clear where this additional capital is going to come from. Although you may think that loan stock might be cheap to raise in the current economic conditions, it is perhaps doubtful if lenders would accept a low return for, say, the next twenty years. A rights issue would have to be serviced by sufficient dividend yield and the company is not retaining any profit currently or building up shareholders' funds.

But these considerations are not so relevant when you are simply going to trade short term and exploit the volatility of the share price. So let us put in some trend lines on the linear chart and see what messages that produces.

Figure 8.11 shows a steady downtrend in the share price since 2007. The 'low' that occurred in March 2009 was 946p and so that sets a benchmark.

Now let us look at the point and figure chart for the period from September 2008 to the middle of July 2009.

Figure 8.12 shows the point and figure chart using a 20p box size, three-box reversal for the period from September 2008 to mid July 2009. You can see a support level marked (line AA), which represents a share price of around 950p. The share price has tested this level twice before in the last ten months.

If the price breaks though this resistance level the chart signal is a very strong sign that the price will continue to fall and you should trade the share by selling short using a CFD where the substantial gearing will enhance your potential profit. You should place a trailing stop-loss limit to control any potential loss should the share price change direction and reverse into an upward movement.

figure 8.11 Severn Trent trading ranges and the support and resistance levels

Source: Updata plc

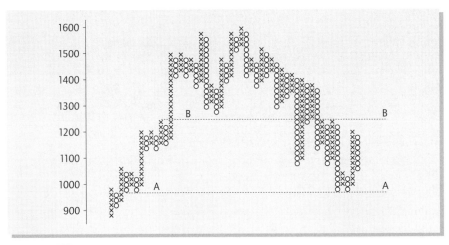

figure 8.12 Severn Trent point and figure chart with support level (AA) and upside resistance level (BB)

The upside resistance level (line BB) is likely to be activated at the price level of around 1,240p. If the current price falls to around 980p and then turns upwards, there is a potential profit of 220 points or more.

Figure 8.12 shows the resistance levels, both up and down. It also illustrates very well how point and figure charts eliminate small movements, called 'noise' by the professionals, which gives you a much clearer picture of the potential upside and downside levels, as well as buy or sell signals.

This is the first time that a book designed for the private investor combines explanations as to how to get the best benefits from using both fundamental and technical analyses when forecasting future share price movements.

In a falling market you will have more opportunities to make money by short selling share prices than by buying to hold for short-term gain. There will usually be more strength in the fall than in the rise. *When the market has established a change of direction* and is generally moving upwards, the reverse is true. There will usually be more upside potential than downside, as is currently the case. *When it turns, do not be in a hurry to invest.* Wait to make sure that the market has turned bullish and that the upward trend is not a brief interlude in a continuing downward movement.

Summary

In this chapter we have demonstrated the effectiveness of using fundamental and technical analysis:

- How to find winners.
- Where to find winners.
- How to reduce your exposure to risk to the minimum.

9

Conclusion

would like to leave you with some general dos and don'ts to reinforce the points made earlier.

1 When the market does turn, and sentiment generally becomes bullish, you must change your tactics. The emphasis will be concentrated more on looking for upward movements in share prices, rather than downward ones. Also, the potential for gain by purchasing shares will be greater than that which will be obtained from short-selling them.

You should still treat every company on its merits and always do your research. There will still be losers, even when the market turns upwards.

You will see the whole market changing, when it does turn, but make sure that the general downtrend has really stopped and that the reversal has become established before you commit yourself. You want to avoid being sucked in by another dead cat bounce.

2 Very often, a share price rises for no obvious reason just before the company announces its results. This is particularly true of those companies that are constituents of the FTSE 100. The reason is because many investors expect an announcement of increased earnings, and they buy the share so the price goes up. (Greed working.)

If you are thinking of selling the share – perhaps because you have made a good profit – that is the time when you should sell. The price nearly always falls immediately after the results have been announced, and the reason is because they are very rarely as good as some shareholders had hoped, so they sell. That brings the price down. That is when you should buy if you were going to buy anyway. Always sell on a rumour and buy on an announcement.

3   For the next few years, the two most lethal threats for of any company, from the largest to the smallest, will be debt and inadequate cash flow. Either one can be crippling; the two together are fatal. You need to monitor these two items constantly in any company whose shares you are intending to hold for twelve months or more.

4   Beware of investing in permanent interest-bearing shares (PIBS) issued by building societies – however attractive their yields may appear to be. They represent unsecured debt and have no voting rights. After the crash of 2008 many investors failed to receive any interest payments and the shares plummeted. In the event of a 'rescue' they would rank below the ordinary shareholders for any compensation and it is doubtful whether they would receive any money at all.

5   Avoid buying shares for long-term investment in companies where the directors pay themselves vast sums by way of remuneration, and/or obscene pension entitlements. If they are going to feather their own nests to such a great extent, it tells you a lot about the contemptuous attitude in which they hold their shareholders. Remember, companies don't run companies – people do. Follow good management that has demonstrated its ability to build shareholder value (ROCE), even when markets have been depressed. Always check the ROCE history back over the last five years at the very least.

6   Never buy a share *only* on the basis of a rumour that a takeover bid is imminent. Any purchase decision *must* be based on fundamental strength, because if the bid does not materialise, the share price will collapse fast.

7   Never get emotionally attached to a company, or a share. If you do, your judgement will become clouded and you will lose money. Companies have to adapt and change along with circumstances, whether they be imposed politically, economically, by the market or by politicians. To do that requires good innovative management with a flexible attitude to change. Companies that do not accept the fact

that markets and consumer preferences are changing all the time will wither and die. Keep a record of profit margins and sales volumes of the companies in your portfolio over the years and these will give you early warnings.

8 If you invest in foreign companies and have to use any currency other than sterling, beware of the relevant exchange rates. Profits can easily be wiped out by adverse currency conversion terms, and losses can also be exacerbated. Don't forget that oil is traded worldwide in US dollars and consequently the relative strength or weakness of that currency against the pound, for example, can influence a share price in ways that have nothing to do with the efficiency or otherwise of the UK company.

9 The futures market exercises a strong influence over a large number of equities listed and traded in London. This influence is growing and it can distort share prices out of all proportion to their true values. There is a widely held body of opinion among the professional financial traders and managers that there are very large inherent dangers that pose enormous threats to the UK economy, particularly from derivatives that have no asset backing. It will pay you to keep an eye on the volume of trades carried out in the futures market for any share in which you have an active interest. If there are very large numbers of futures being bought, or sold, try to find out what the reasons are.

10 When you have done all your homework and you are satisfied that you have identified an opportunity to make a profit with minimum risks, make a substantial investment and then watch it closely. If, at any time, you start to have a doubt – get out. There is no magic wand to wave that will make money for you easily. It takes hard work and your commitments require constant supervision while your capital is invested, and therefore at risk. But, as fishermen say, 'You won't catch a fish unless your fly is in the water', so being at risk is part of the game.

This book has been written to help you understand how to recognise opportunities for making money, and what analyses to do to satisfy yourself that you have evaluated as many risks as possible so that you stand a much better than even chance of winning. Run your profits until they turn, then sell. If you can win consistently seven times out of ten, you will be doing well.

Good luck.

Appendix 1

Company financial information

A.G. Barr plc

Preliminary results for the year ended 31 January 2009

A.G. Barr plc, the soft drinks group, announces its preliminary results for the 12 months to 31 January 2009.

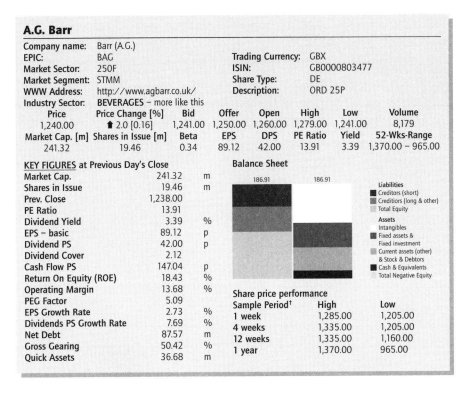

A.G. Barr

Company name:	Barr (A.G.)							
EPIC:	BAG			Trading Currency:	GBX			
Market Sector:	250F			ISIN:	GB0000803477			
Market Segment:	STMM			Share Type:	DE			
WWW Address:	http://www.agbarr.co.uk/			Description:	ORD 25P			
Industry Sector:	BEVERAGES – more like this							

Price	Price Change [%]	Bid	Offer	Open	High	Low	Volume
1,240.00	↑ 2.0 [0.16]	1,241.00	1,250.00	1,260.00	1,279.00	1,241.00	8,179

Market Cap. [m]	Shares in Issue [m]	Beta	EPS	DPS	PE Ratio	Yield	52-Wks-Range
241.32	19.46	0.34	89.12	42.00	13.91	3.39	1,370.00 – 965.00

KEY FIGURES at Previous Day's Close

Market Cap.	241.32	m
Shares in Issue	19.46	m
Prev. Close	1,238.00	
PE Ratio	13.91	
Dividend Yield	3.39	%
EPS – basic	89.12	p
Dividend PS	42.00	p
Dividend Cover	2.12	
Cash Flow PS	147.04	p
Return On Equity (ROE)	18.43	%
Operating Margin	13.68	%
PEG Factor	5.09	
EPS Growth Rate	2.73	%
Dividends PS Growth Rate	7.69	%
Net Debt	87.57	m
Gross Gearing	50.42	%
Quick Assets	36.68	m

Balance Sheet

186.91   186.91

Liabilities
- Creditors (short)
- Creditiors (long & other)
- Total Equity

Assets
- Intangibles
- Fixed assets & Fixed investment
- Current assets (other) & Stock & Debtors
- Cash & Equivalents
- Total Negative Equity

Share price performance

Sample Period[+]	High	Low
1 week	1,285.00	1,205.00
4 weeks	1,335.00	1,205.00
12 weeks	1,335.00	1,160.00
1 year	1,370.00	965.00

Net Working Capital	12.30	m
Intangibles/Fixed Assets	56.60	%
Turnover PS	871.97	p
Pre-Tax Profit PS	119.26	p
Retained Profit PS	48.67	p
Cash PS	34.32	p
Net Cash PS	−165.64	p
Net Tangible Asset Value PS*	81.48	p
Net Asset Value PS	476.15	p
Spread	9.00 (0.72%)	

* Calculation based on Ordinary Capital figure as contained in last annual report, and the most recent shares in issue figure. Therefore the ratio might be exposed to inaccuracies.

Share price performance previous 5 years

© www.advfn.com

DEEPER ANALYSIS

Investment Ratios

(Market value analysis) as previous day's close

PQ Ratio	12.71	
PE Ratio	13.91	
Tobin's Q Ratio	1.55	
Tobin's Q Ratio (excl. intangibles)	2.16	
Dividend Yield	3.39	%
Market-to-Book Ratio	2.60	
Price-to-Pre-Tax Profit PS	10.40	
Price-to-Retained Profit PS	25.48	
Price-to-Cash Flow PS	8.43	
Price-to-Sales PS	1.42	
Price-to-Net Tangible Asset Value PS	15.22	
Price-to-Cash PS	36.13	
Net Working Capital PS	63.18	
Price Pct to Working Capital PS	19.63	%
Earnings Yield	7.19	%
Average PE	14.39	
Years in average	5	
PE to PE average	96.71	%

Operating Ratios

Profitability Ratios)

Return On Capital Employed (ROCE)	15.68	%
Return On Assets (ROA)	10.99	%
Net Profit Margin	10.06	%
Assets Turnover	1.09	
Return On Equity (ROE)	18.43	%
Return On Investment (ROI)	14.04	%
Dividend Payout Ratio	47.13	%
Plowback Ratio	52.87	%
Growth from Plowback Ratio	10.18	%
Net Income Of Revenues	5.58	%

(Asset Utilisation Multiples)

Shareholders Equity Turnover	1.91	
Fixed Assets Turnover	1.70	
Current Assets Turnover	3.06	
Net Working Capital Turnover	-	
Inventory Turnover	12.63	

(Other Operating Ratios)

Total Assets-to-Sales	0.92	
Debtors-to-Sales	15.65	%
Debt Collection Period	57.11	Days

Financial Ratios

(Leverage Ratios)

Debt Ratio	37.39	%
Debt-to-Equity Ratio	0.60	
Debt-to-Equity Ratio (excl. Intgbl)	3.49	
Debt-to-Equity Market Value	0.23	
Net Gearing	46.85	%
Net Gearing (excl. Intangibles)	79.53	%
Gross Gearing	50.42	%
Gross Gearing (excl. Intangibles)	85.60	%
Gearing Under 1 Year	20.82	%
Gearing Under 1 Year (excl. Intgbl)	35.34	%
Assets/Equity	2.02	
Cash/Equity	7.21	

(Liquidity Ratios)

Net Working Capital to Total Assets	6.58	%
Current Ratio	1.32	
Quick Ratio (Acid Test)	0.94	
Liquidity Ratio	0.17	
Cash & Equiv/Current Assets	13.04	%

(Solvency Ratios)

Enterprise Value	289.97	m
CFO/Sales	0.17	
CFO/Attributable Profit	1.68	
CFO/Assets	0.15	
CFO/Debt	0.30	
Total Debt/Equity Market Value	0.39	
Total Debt/Sales	0.56	
Total Debt/Pre-Tax Profit	4.06	
Total Debt	94.25	m
Total Debt/Net Current Assets	7.66	%

(Dodds – Graham Ratios)

3 yr Compound Earnings Growth	8.56	%
5 yr Compound Earnings Growth	7.32	%
10 yr Compound Earnings Growth	6.87	%
Earn drops > 5% in 10 yrs	1	

Beta coefficients

| Beta (60-Mnth) | Beta (36-Mnth) |
| 0.3423 | 0.3293 |

Alpha coefficients

| Alpha (60-Mnth) | Alpha (36-Mnth) |
| 0.0118 | 0.0102 |

FUNDAMENTALS

Profit and Loss Account

	28 Jan 2006 (GBP)		27 Jan 2007 (GBP)		26 Jan 2008 (GBP)		31 Jan 2009 (GBP)	
turnover	128.76	100.00%	141.88	100.00%	148.38	100.00%	169.70	100.00% m
pre tax profit	17.38	13.50%	16.35	11.53%	20.83	14.04%	23.21	13.68% m
attributable profit	12.25	9.52%	13.19	9.30%	16.84	11.35%	17.08	10.06% m
retained profit	6.63	5.15%	7.11	5.01%	10.09	6.80%	9.47	5.58% m
eps − basic	65.06		69.65		86.75		89.12	
eps − diluted	63.87		68.15		85.65		88.16	
dividends per share	31.75		35.00		39.00		42.00	

Balance Sheet

	28 Jan 2006 (GBP)	27 Jan 2007 (GBP)	26 Jan 2008 (GBP)	31 Jan 2009 (GBP)

Liabilities
■ Creditors (short)
■ Creditors (long & other)
▨ Total Equity
Assets
▨ Intangibles
■ Fixed assets &
  Fixed investment
▨ Current assets (other)
  & Stock & Debtors
■ Cash & Equivalents
  Total Negative Equity

| | 105.85 | 105.85 | 118.63 | 118.63 | 123.70 | 123.70 | 186.91 | 186.91 |

	28 Jan 2006 (GBP)		27 Jan 2007 (GBP)		26 Jan 2008 (GBP)		31 Jan 2009 (GBP)	
ASSETS								
■ fixed assets	42.34	40.00%	52.28	44.07%	53.37	43.15%	58.86	31.49% m
■ intangibles	-	-%	9.74	8.21%	10.66	8.61%	76.81	41.09% m
■ fixed investments	0.75	0.71%	0.70	0.59%	-	-%	0.03	0.02% m
■ current assets − other	0.94	0.89%	-	-%	3.47	2.80%	2.86	1.53% m
▨ stocks	8.27	7.82%	11.41	9.62%	12.34	9.98%	14.53	7.77% m
▨ debtors	22.14	20.92%	25.41	21.42%	25.97	20.99%	27.14	14.52% m
cash & securities	31.41	29.68%	19.10	16.10%	17.90	14.47%	6.68	3.57% m
TOTAL	105.85	100%	118.63	100%	123.70	100%	186.91	100% m
LIABILITIES								
■ creditors − short	24.05	22.72%	31.10	26.21%	28.45	23.00%	38.92	20.81% m
■ creditors − long	16.86	15.93%	16.16	13.62%	10.47	8.47%	55.33	29.60% m
■ creditors − other	-	-%	-	-%	-	-%	-	-% m
■ subordinated loans	-	-%	-	-%	-	-%	-	-% m
▨ insurance funds	-	-%	-	-%	-	-%	-	-% m
TOTAL	40.90	38.64%	47.25	39.83%	38.92	31.46%	94.25	50.42% m
EQUITY								
■ ord. cap. reserves	64.94	61.36%	71.38	60.17%	84.78	68.54%	92.67	49.58% m
▨ prefs. minorities	-	-%	-	-%	-	-%	-	-% m
TOTAL	64.94	61.36%	71.38	60.17%	84.78	68.54%	92.67	49.58% m
OTHER								
NAV Basic	-		-		-		-	
NAV Diluted	-		-		-		-	

Cash Flow Statement

	28 Jan 2006 (GBP)	27 Jan 2007 (GBP)	26 Jan 2008 (GBP)	31 Jan 2009 (GBP)
Operating CF	14.01	16.76	17.81	28.62 m
Pre-Financing CF	3.47	−5.74	6.37	−39.66 m
Retained CF	−3.55	−12.32	−1.20	−11.22 m

figure A1   A.G. Barr financial information   Source: ADVFN (www.advfn.com)

Key points

- Profit on ordinary activities before tax and exceptional items increased by **9.7%** to **£23.4m** (2008 – £21.3m).

- Turnover increased by **14.4%** to **£169.7m** (2008 – £148.4m).

- The underlying business showed excellent growth up **6.6%** after adjusting for the acquisition of the Rubicon business and the 53rd week.

- Proposed final dividend of **30.4p** per share to give a proposed total dividend for the year of **42.0p** per share, an increase of **7.7%** over the previous year.

- IRN-BRU and Diet IRN-BRU revenue increased by almost 8% – growing in all territories.

- Core carbonate brands and still juice brands both grew well ahead of the market.

- Cash flow remained strong generating **£18m** of free cash flow in the period.

- Lower than anticipated net debt of **£31.3m** and long term banking facilities in place.

- Integration of Rubicon business into core operations is well under way.

- Orangina Schweppes Group agrees new 6-year Orangina franchise deal.

Commenting, Roger White, chief executive said:

'Over the last 12 months we have seen substantial growth in both sales revenues and profit despite a further summer of poor weather and the difficult economic environment. We are now benefiting from our continued investments in brands and people as well as the restructuring activity which we have undertaken in recent years. Despite the challenging economic climate our business is financially strong and well capable of continuing to deliver sustainable growth.'

Appendix 2

Britvic plc interim results

Britvic plc ('Britvic') today announces its interim results for the 28 weeks ended 12 April 2009 ('the period'). Numbers in the table below are all quoted before exceptional items.

	28 weeks ended 12 April 2009 (£m)	28 weeks ended 13 April 2008 (£m)	% change
Group revenue:	483.2	454.7	6.3
GB Carbonates	*204.4*	*185.4*	*10.2*
GB Stills	*168.7*	*161.8*	*4.3*
Ireland	*101.1*	*99.5*	*1.6*
International	*9.0*	*8.0*	*12.5*
GB & international operating profit	31.9	27.1	17.7
Britvic Ireland operating profit	0.0	4.3	(100.0)
Group Operating Profit	31.9	31.4	1.6
Group operating profit margin	*6.6%*	*6.9%*	*(30)bps*
Group profit before tax	20.0	17.2	16.3
Group profit after tax	14.8	13.0	13.8
Basic earnings per share	6.9p	6.1p	13.1
Interim dividend per share	4.1p	3.8p	7.9
EBITDA(2)	53.5	55.2	(3.1)
Free cash flow(1)	(24.6)	(10.5)	(134.3)
Adjusted net group debt(3)	(442.7)	(454.1)	2.5

Britvic

Company name:	Britvic					
EPIC:	BVIC		Trading Currency:	GBX		
Market Sector:	F25F		ISIN:	GB00B0N8QD54		
Market Segment:	STMM		Share Type:	DE		
WWW Address:	http://www.britvic.com/britvic.home			Description:		ORD 20P
Industry Sector:	BEVERAGES – more like this					

Price	Price Change [%]	Bid	Offer	Open	High	Low	Volume
280.00	⬆ 5.0 [1.82]	280.00	280.50	273.00	282.00	273.00	347,429

Market Cap. [m]	Shares in Issue [m]	Beta	EPS	DPS	PE Ratio	Yield	52-Wks-Range
605.17	216.13	1.14	14.90	11.00	18.79	3.93	311.75 – 161.25

KEY FIGURES at Previous Day's Close

Market Cap.	605.17	m
Shares in Issue	216.13	m
Prev. Close	275.00	
PE Ratio	18.79	
Dividend Yield	3.93	%
EPS – basic	14.90	p
Dividend PS	11.00	p
Dividend Cover	1.35	
Cash Flow PS	66.26	p
Return On Equity (ROE)	341.94	%
Operating Margin	5.59	%
PEG Factor	−0.70	
EPS Growth Rate	−26.96	%
Dividends PS Growth Rate	-	%
Net Debt	717.80	m
Gross Gearing	98.75	%
Quick Assets	172.80	m
Net Working Capital	−44.30	m
Intangibles / Fixed Assets	50.82	%
Turnover PS	428.68	p
Pre-Tax Profit PS	23.97	p
Retained Profit PS	3.29	p
Cash PS	6.57	p
Net Cash PS	−116.74	p
Net Tangible Asset Value PS *	−117.75	p
Net Asset Value PS	4.30	p
Spread	0.50 (0.18%)	

* Calculation based on Ordinary Capital figure as contained in last annual report, and the most recent shares in issue figure. Therefore the ratio might be exposed to inaccuracies.

Balance Sheet

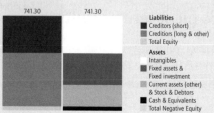

741.30   741.30

Liabilities
- Creditors (short)
- Creditors (long & other)
- Total Equity

Assets
- Intangibles
- Fixed assets & Fixed investment
- Current assets (other) & Stock & Debtors
- Cash & Equivalents
- Total Negative Equity

For Sector Balance Sheet comparisons Click here

Share price performance

Sample Period †	High	Low
1 week	282.00	253.25
4 weeks	285.75	253.25
12 weeks	311.75	240.00
1 year	311.75	161.25

Share price performance previous 5 years

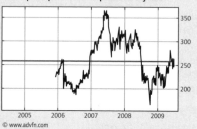

© www.advfn.com

DEEPER ANALYSIS

Investment Ratios
(Market value analysis) at previous days's close

PQ Ratio	10.77
PE Ratio	18.79
Tobin's Q Ratio	0.84
Tobin's Q Ratio (excl. intangibles)	1.31
Dividend Yield	3.93 %
Market-to-Book Ratio	65.07
Price-to-Pre-Tax profit PS	11.68
Price-to-Retained Profit PS	85.23
Price-to-Cash Flow PS	4.23
Price-to-Sales PS	0.65
Price-to-Net Tangible Asset Value PS	−2.38

Financial Ratios
(Leverage Ratios)

Debt Ratio	98.04	%
Debt-to-Equity Ratio	50.05	
Debt-to-Equity Ratio (excl. Intgbl)	−1.83	
Debt-to-Equity Market Value	0.77	
Net Gearing	96.83	%
Net Gearing (excl. Intangibles)	150.32	%
Gross Gearing	98.75	%
Gross Gearing (excl. Intangibles)	153.30	%
Gearing Under 1 Year	35.95	%
Gearing Under 1 Year (excl. Intgbl)	55.81	%
Assets/Equity	79.71	

Price-to-Cash PS	42.62	Cash/Equity	152.69
Net Working Capital PS	−20.50	(Liquidity Ratios)	
Price Pct to Working Capital PS	−13.66 %	Net Working Capital to Total Assets	−5.98 %
Earnings Yield	5.32 %	Current Ratio	0.83
Average PE	16.96	Quick Ratio (Acid Test)	0.65
Years in average	3	Liquidity Ratio	0.05
PE to PE average	110.78 %	Cash & Equiv/Current Assets	6.39 %
Operating Ratios		(Solvency Ratios)	
Profitability Ratios)		Enterprise Value	1,056.47 m
Return On Capital Employed (ROCE)	10.91 %	CFO/Sales	0.15
Return On Assets (ROA)	4.43 %	CFO/Attributable Profit	4.50
Net Profit Margin	3.43 %	CFO/Assets	0.19
Assets Turnover	1.29	CFO/Debt	0.20
Return On Equity (ROE)	314.94 %	Total Debt/Equity Market Value	1.21
Return On Investment (ROI)	6.72 %	Total Debt/Sales	0.79
Dividend Payout Ratio	73.83 %	Total Debt/Pre-Tax Profit	14.12
Plowback Ratio	26.17 %	Total Debt	732.00 m
Growth from Plowback Ratio	332.94 %	Total Debt/Net Current Assets	−16.52 %
Net Income Of Revenues	0.77 %	(Dodds – Graham Ratios)	
(Asset Utilisation Multiples)		3 yr Compound Earnings Growth	9.98 %
Shareholders Equity Turnover	370.60	5 yr Compound Earnings Growth	- %
Fixed Assets Turnover	1.84	10 yr Compound Earnings Growth	- %
Current Assets Turnover	4.31	Earn drops > 5% in 10 yrs	2
Net Working Capital Turnover	-	Beta coefficients	
Inventory Turnover	19.57	Beta (60-Mnth) Beta (36-Mnth)	
(Other Operating Ratios)		1.1368 1.2447	
Total Assets-to-Sales	0.77	Alpha coefficients	
Debtors-to-Sales	15.25 %	Alpha (60-Mnth) Alpha (36-Mnth)	
Debt Collection Period	55.65 Days	0.0138 0.0239	

FUNDAMENTALS

Profit and Loss Account

	02 Oct 2005 (GBP)		01 Oct 2006 (GBP)		30 Sep 2007 (GBP)		28 Sep 2008 (GBP)	
turnover	698.20	100.00%	677.90	100.00%	716.30	100.00%	926.50	100.00% m
pre tax profit	64.20	9.20%	36.50	5.38%	55.60	7.76%	51.80	5.59% m
attributable profit	43.40	6.22%	24.20	3.57%	42.50	5.93%	31.80	3.43% m
retained profit	43.40	6.22%	−29.10	−4.29%	20.30	2.83%	7.10	0.77% m
eps – basic	20.20		11.20		20.40		14.90	
eps – diluted	20.20		11.20		20.40		14.60	
dividends per share	-		10.00		11.00		11.00	

Balance Sheet

	02 Oct 2005 (GBP)	01 Oct 2006 (GBP)	30 Sep 2007 (GBP)	28 Sep 2008 (GBP)

| | 492.40   492.40 | 582.50   582.50 | 690.30   690.30 | 741.30   741.30 |

Liabilities
■ Creditors (short)
■ Creditors (long & other)
▨ Total Equity

Assets
Intangibles
■ Fixed assets &
Fixed investment
▨ Current assets (other)
& Stock & Debtors
■ Cash & Equivalents
Total Negative Equity

	02 Oct 2005 (GBP)	01 Oct 2006 (GBP)	30 Sep 2007 (GBP)	28 Sep 2008 (GBP)

ASSETS

■ fixed assets	231.50	47.01%	218.20	46.71%	225.20	32.42%	228.10	30.77% m
■ intangibles	96.70	19.64%	95.40	20.42%	247.40	35.62%	263.80	35.59% m
■ fixed investments	5.10	1.04%	2.40	0.51%	14.70	2.12%	27.20	3.67% m
▨ current assets – other	-	-%	-	-%	4.80	0.69%	5.90	0.80% m

	28 Jan 2006		27 Jan 2007		26 Jan 2008		31 Jan 2009		
■ stocks	37.90	7.70%	31.70	6.79%	45.30	6.52%	49.40	6.60%	m
■ debtors	101.80	20.67%	99.60	21.32%	129.80	18.69%	152.70	20.60%	m
□ cash & securities	19.40	3.94%	19.80	4.24%	27.40	3.94%	14.20	1.92%	m
TOTAL	492.40	100%	467.10	100%	694.60	100%	741.30	100%	m
LIABILITIES									
■ creditors – short	166.30	33.77%	171.40	36.69%	223.20	32.13%	266.50	35.95%	m
■ creditors – long	303.90	61.72%	353.40	75.66%	467.10	67.25%	465.50	62.80%	m
■ creditors – other	-	-%	-	-%	-	-%	-	-%	m
■ subordinated loans	-	-%	-	-%	-	-%	-	-%	m
▨ insurance funds	-	-%	-	-%	-	-%	-	-%	m
TOTAL	470.20	95.49%	524.80	112.35%	690.30	99.38%	732.00	98.75%	m
EQUITY									
■ ord. cap. reserves	22.20	4.51%	57.70	12.35%	−4.30	−0.62%	9.30	1.25%	m
▨ prefs. minorities	-	-%	-	-%	-	-%	-	-%	m
TOTAL	22.20	4.51%	57.70	12.35%	−4.30	−0.62%	9.30	1.25%	m
OTHER									
NAV Basic	-		-		-		-		
NAV Diluted	-		-		-		-		

Cash Flow Statement

	28 Jan 2006 (GBP)	27 Jan 2007 (GBP)	26 Jan 2008 (GBP)	31 Jan 2009 (GBP)	
Operating CF	56.00	88.60	106.20	143.20	m
Pre-Financing CF	0.30	55.80	−69.80	−91.60	m
Retained CF	−7.60	−2.00	8.10	−13.60	m

figure A2 Britvic financial information

Source: ADVFN (www.advfn.com)

Appendix 3

Severn Trent plc interim results

Severn Trent

Company name:	Severn Trent
Company Description:	Supply of water and sewage services worldwide; Biffa Waste Services offer integrated waste management services in the UK and Belgium; Severn Trent Systems provides a range of utility management information systems, network modelling and software solutions for electricity, natural gas and water utilities worldwide. Severn Trent Water International provides water and waste water management expertise in Western Europe and North America; Severn Trent Technology develops and markets new and existing technologies in water and waste water management; Severn Trent Property develops facilities in the UK for distribution, retail and industrial sectors

EPIC:	SVT		Trading Currency:	GBX
Market Sector:	FS10		ISIN:	GB00B1FH8J72
Market Segment:	SET1		Share Type:	DE
WWW Address:	http://www.severn-trent.com/		Description:	ORD 97 17/19P
Industry Sector:	GAS WATER & UTILITIES – more like this			

Price	Price Change [%]	Bid	Offer	Open	High	Low	Volume
1,105.00	⬇ −5.0 [−0.45]	1,106.00	1,107.00	1,114.00	1,123.00	1,100.00	787,209

Market Cap. [m]	Shares in Issue [m]	Beta	EPS	DPS	PE Ratio	Yield	52-Wks-Range
2,612.97	236.47	0.62	−24.60	67.34	-	6.09	1,465.00 – 946.00

KEY FIGURES at Previous Day's Close

Market Cap.	2,612.97	m
Share in Issue	236.47	m
Prev. Close	1,110.00	
PE Ratio	-	
Dividend Yield	6.09	%
EPS – basic	−24.60	p
Dividend PS	67.34	p
Dividend Cover	-	
Cash Flow PS	272.13	p
Return On Equity (ROE)	−6.11	%
Operating Margin	10.21	%
PEG Factor	-	
EPS Growth Rate	−127.42	%
Dividends PS Growth Rate	2.61	%
Net Debt	5,925.50	m
Gross Gearing	87.40	%
Quick Assets	1,129.60	m
Net Working Capital	370.20	m

Balance Sheet

7,555.50   7,555.50

Liabilities
- Creditors (short)
- Creditiors (long & other)
- Total Equity

Assets
- Intangibles
- Fixed assets & Fixed investment
- Current assets (other) & Stock & Debtors
- Cash & Equivalents
- Total Negative Equity

For Sector Balance sheet comparisons Click here

Share price performance

Sample Period †	High	Low
1 week	1,130.00	1,091.00
4 weeks	1,201.00	1,088.00
12 weeks	1,201.00	979.50
1 year	1,465.00	946.00

Intangibles / Fixed Assets	2.89	%
Turnover PS	694.47	p
Pre-Tax Profit PS	70.88	p
Retained Profit PS	−91.60	p
Cash PS	286.68	p
Net Cash PS	−47.41	p
Net Tangible Asset Value PS *	322.03	p
Net Asset Value PS	402.63	p
Spread	1.00 (0.09%)	

* Calculations based on Ordinary Capital figure as contained in last annual report, and the most recent shares in issue figure. Therefore the ratio might be exposed to inaccuracies.

Share price performance previous 5 years

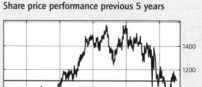
© www.advfn.com

DEEPER ANALYSIS

Investment Ratios
(Market value analysis) as previous day's close

PQ Ratio	3.74
PE Ratio	-
Tobin's Q Ratio	0.36
Tobin's Q Ratio (excl. intangibles)	0.37
Dividend Yield	6.09 %
Market-to-Book Ratio	2.76
Price-to-Pre-Tax Profit PS	15.59
Price-to-Retained Profit PS	−12.06
Price-to-Cash Flow PS	4.06
Price-to-Sales PS	1.59
Price-to-Net Tangible Asset Value PS	3.40
Price-to-Cash PS	3.85
Net Working Capital PS	156.55
Price Pct to Working Capital PS	7.06 %
Earnings Yield	- %
Average PE	15.02
Years in average	4
PE to PE average	- %

Operating Ratios
Profitability Ratios)

Return On Capital Employed (ROCE)	2.48	%
Return On Assets (ROA)	−0.79	%
Net Profit Margin	−3.52	%
Assets Turnover	0.22	
Return On Equity (ROE)	−6.11	%
Return On Investment (ROI)	−0.90	%
Dividend Payout Ratio	-	%
Plowback Ratio	100.00	%
Growth from Plowback Ratio	-	%
Net Income Of Revenues	−13.19	%

(Asset Utilisation Multiples)

Shareholders Equity Turnover	1.53
Fixed Assets Turnover	0.27
Current Assets Turnover	1.44
Net Working Capital Turnover	-
Inventory Turnover	59.29

(Other Operating Ratios)

Total Assets-to-Sales	4.45	
Debtors-to-Sales	26.83	%
Debt Collection Period	97.93	Days

Financial Ratios
(Leverage Ratios)

Debt Ratio	85.93	%
Debt-to-Equity Ratio	6.11	
Debt-to-Equity Ratio (excl. Intgbl)	7.57	
Debt-to-Equity Market Value	2.22	
Net Gearing	78.43	%
Net Gearing (excl. Intangibles)	80.39	%
Gross Gearing	87.40	%
Gross Gearing (excl. Intangibles)	89.59	%
Gearing Under 1 Year	10.49	%
Gearing Under 1 Year (excl. Intgbl)	10.72	%
Assets/Equity	7.94	
Cash/Equity	71.20	

(Liquidity Ratios)

Net Working Capital to Total Assets	4.90	%
Current Ratio	1.47	
Quick Ratio (Acid Test)	1.43	
Liquidity Ratio	0.86	
Cash & Equiv/Current Assets	58.43	%

(Solvency Ratios)

Enterprise Value	7,754.47	m
CFO/Sales	0.39	
CFO/Attributable Profit	-	
CFO/Assets	0.09	
CFO/Debt	0.10	
Total Debt/Equity Market Value	2.53	
Total Debt/Sales	4.02	
Total Debt/Pre-Tax Profit	39.40	
Total Debt	6,603.40	m
Total Debt/Net Current Assets	17.84	%

(Dodds − Graham Ratios)

3 yr Compound Earnings Growth	-	%
5 yr Compound Earnings Growth	-	%
10 yr Compound Earnings Growth	-	%
Earn drops > 5% in 10 yrs	5	

Beta coefficients

Beta (60-Mnth)	Beta (36-Mnth)
0.6165	0.6280

Alpha coefficients

Alpha (60-Mnth)	Alpha (36-Mnth)
0.0071	0.0054

FUNDAMENTALS
Profit and Loss Account

	31 Mar 2006 (GBP)		31 Mar 2007 (GBP)		31 Mar 2008 (GBP)		31 Mar 2009 (GBP)	
turnover	1,455.30	100.00%	1,480.20	100.00%	1,552.40	100.00%	1,642.20	100.00% m
pre tax profit	177.80	12.22%	325.50	21.99%	192.40	12.39%	167.60	10.21% m
attributable profit	221.60	15.23%	267.10	18.04%	209.50	13.50%	−57.80	−3.52% m
retained profit	−12.70	0.87%	−472.40	−31.91%	62.20	4.01%	216.60	−13.19% m
eps − basic	95.90		114.70		89.70		−24.60	
eps − diluted	95.10		113.60		89.00		−24.60	
dividends per share	51.13		61.45		65.63		67.34	

Balance Sheet

	31 Mar 2006 (GBP)	31 Mar 2007 (GBP)	31 Mar 2008 (GBP)	31 Mar 2009 (GBP)

Liabilities
- Creditors (short)
- Creditors (long & other)
- Total Equity

Assets
- Intangibles
- Fixed assets &
- Fixed investment
- Current assets (other)
- & Stock & Debtors
- Cash & Equivalents
- Total Negative Equity

Bar chart values: 7,126.10 | 7,126.10 | 6,248.90 | 6,248.90 | 7,062.80 | 7,062.80 | 7,555.50 | 7,555.50

	31 Mar 2006 (GBP)		31 Mar 2007 (GBP)		31 Mar 2008 (GBP)		31 Mar 2009 (GBP)	
ASSETS								
■ fixed assets	5,743.10	80.59%	5,521.10	88.35%	5,731.20	81.15%	5,980.10	79.15% m
■ intangibles	618.70	8.68%	150.30	2.41%	157.40	2.23%	184.60	2.44% m
■ fixed investments	33.50	0.47%	23.20	0.37%	55.60	0.79%	230.60	3.05% m
■ current assets − other	41.50	0.58%	-	-%	-	-%	4.60	0.06% m
■ stocks	54.40	0.76%	22.40	0.36%	24.80	0.35%	30.60	0.41% m
▨ debtors	482.50	6.76%	387.10	6.19%	434.10	6.15%	447.10	5.92% m
cash & securities	153.40	2.15%	144.80	2.32%	659.70	9.34%	677.90	8.97% m
TOTAL	7,126.10	100%	6,248.90	100%	7,062.80	100%	7,555.50	100% m
LIABILITIES								
■ creditors − short	1,570.60	22.04%	1,112.20	17.80%	974.60	13.80%	790.00	10.46% m
■ creditors − long	3,656.50	51.31%	3,999.40	64.00%	4,883.00	69.14%	5,813.40	76.94% m
■ creditors − other	-	-%	-	-%	-	-%	-	-% m
▨ subordinated loans	-	-%	-	-%	-	-%	-	-% m
▨ insurance funds	-	-%	-	-%	-	-%	-	-% m
TOTAL	5,227.10	73.35%	5,111.60	81.80%	5,857.60	82.94%	6,603.40	87.40% m
EQUITY								
■ ord cap. Reserves	1,896.40	26.61%	1,134.20	18.15%	1,201.00	17.00%	946.10	12.52% m
▨ prefs. Minorities	2.60	0.04%	3.10	0.05%	4.20	0.06%	6.00	0.08% m
TOTAL	1,899.00	26.65%	1,137.30	18.20%	1,205.20	17.06%	952.10	12.60% m
OTHER								
NAV Basic	-		-		-		-	
NAV Diluted	-		-		-		-	

figure A3 Severn Trent financial information

Source: ADVFN (www.advfn.com)

Index